# ONE-TRACK MIND

# ONE-TRACK MIND

## 15 Ways to Amplify Your Child's Special Interest

Andrea Moriarty

Cover photo: Copyright 2015 Spenser Heaps, Daily Herald

ISBN: 0692533192
ISBN 13: 9780692533192
Library of Congress Control Number: 2015913254
JAM Ink, Solana Beach, California

*This book is dedicated to all the parents in the trenches, with a prayer that you will be strengthened to fulfill your purpose.*

# Table of Contents

# Introduction

*God made man because he loves stories.*

—RABBI NACHMAN OF BRATZLEV

remember a particular Mom's Night Out—with myself. My husband Jim and I felt like transients with our five-year-old twins, Allie and Reid, in a temporary apartment, waiting for our kitchen to be remodeled after relocating for the third time in three years. Maybe Jim heard a child's deafening scream as he drove toward our unit, glanced at my copious, frantic notes on tile, appliances, and every autism service provider in San Diego County, or maybe dinner was makeshift for the third night in a row. Somehow the exasperation in my eyes prompted him to insist, "Go grab a coffee or something. You need a break."

Though the predictable order of a grocery store with its mind-numbing Muzak might have sufficed, I ended up in a bookstore, combing the shelves to prove C. S. Lewis right when he wrote, "We read to know we're not alone." I wondered, *Is there a friendly, honest, genuine, encouraging book out there somewhere?* I needed to know I wasn't alone. I yearned to hear how others coped with the physical, mental, emotional, and spiritual demands this kid—my son, whom I loved so much—presented me with on a daily, hourly, and minute-by-minute basis. His hyperactivity, hypersensitivity, and autism diagnosis had thrown us into a tailspin that threatened to never end.

I browsed a long time before I found her, but I knew she was mine, turning up in the far corner of the discount, off-brand seller. I read *Changed by a Child*, a book of short, devotional-style essays, cover to cover as if it were a mystery novel. Then I dog-eared the pages and annotated it like a Bible. The author, Barbara Gill, knew exactly what I was thinking and feeling. She seemed to know what was coming down the pike, too. I saved sections that didn't resonate right then. I trusted her enough to know they would matter later. I wasn't alone anymore.

I hope you will find this book at the right time and believe my promise of better days. You are not alone. The challenge of raising an atypical learner—whatever the diagnosis—is possible, even though it is difficult. After twenty years of firsthand experience, I've developed some habits I know I didn't have at the beginning. For example, I bite my lower left lip in perpetual quandary and pull out my hair in a gesture that is part nervousness and part self-soothing. Indeed, I have been changed by a child, but not just in undesirable ways. For the better, I am no longer a perfectionistic, overachieving control freak. I think I am more compassionate, humble, and wise.

—❧—

At our wedding nearly thirty years ago, a children's choir sang and my husband and I chose a passage from *The Velveteen Rabbit* by Margery Williams to be read in addition to the scripture readings.

*"Real isn't how you are made," said the Skin Horse. "It's a thing that happens to you. When a child loves you for a long, long time, not just to play with, but REALLY loves you, then you become Real."*

*"Does it hurt?" asked the Rabbit.*

*"Sometimes," said the Skin Horse, for he was always truthful. "When you are Real you don't mind being hurt."*

*"Does it happen all at once, like being wound up," he asked, "or bit by bit?"*

*"It doesn't happen all at once," said the Skin Horse. "You become. It takes a long time. That's why it doesn't happen often to people who break easily, or have sharp edges, or who have to be carefully kept. Generally, by the time you are Real, most of your hair has been loved off, and your eyes drop out and you get loose in the joints and very shabby. But these things don't matter at all, because once you are Real you can't be ugly, except to people who don't understand."*

Whatever we were anticipating that day, it turns out the all-consuming process of raising a child with special needs is what has made us most *real*. A close friend says of their similar experience, "I don't think I'd like the person I would have become if it weren't for Josie [their daughter with special needs]."

My singular ambition in life was to be a mom. Somewhere along the line, parenting got more complicated than I imagined though. Late nights of inconsolable screaming, years of outwitting a whirling top, days of pretending to be normal, hours in clinics and medical offices, and more recommendations than one person can implement in a lifetime had turned it into full-time overtime. It became a spiritual quest that included facing my own inabilities, fears, failures, need for help, arrogance, prejudice, and lies. Potty training after age seven can do that.

Still to this day, it employs resourcefulness, persistence, forgiveness, and patience from a deeper reservoir than I knew existed, which is where God comes in. As if I were the autistic child, not Reid, God has guided me through tricky transitions, advocated for needs I didn't know I had, changed my world to help me cope, soothed me through a meltdown, protected me from danger, followed me when I wandered off, and repeated truths I couldn't comprehend until they started to make sense. Without spoken words, He has engaged and motivated me as if He were the parent in the trenches, not me. He has loved me when I was not lovable, waited out my defiance, refused to take my avoidance personally, and proven He is for me. He has parented me with the tenderness and authority of an Almighty Father and more passion than a supermom. The good news is that He is willing to do that for you too.

As Reid does with me, I tune in and out of my relationship with God, but when I'm at my best, firing on all cylinders, I get a taste of the glory of heaven. That may be what life is for anyway: a dress rehearsal for eternity. I am more prepared for heaven because of the practice I've had parenting Reid. As if banging my head against a wall, I have ranted and raved at God for things I thought I must have. Unfazed, He decided what was best, and now I see that love does not mean removing challenges. Love can be concurrent with pain. As Mister Rogers put it, "Love is an active noun like struggle. To love someone is to strive to accept that person exactly the way he or she is, right here and now." As I have persisted to connect with my nearly nonverbal son, a mostly inaudible God has connected with me in tender and personal ways.

What you are doing as a parent matters, so keep calm and carry on; you can do this. Your child was made by the creator, on purpose not by accident. In Isaiah 46:4 He promises, "I made you, and I will care for you." There is a plan for your child. I believe the challenges are not a detour but actually a vital part of the process. We were created to give and receive love. What's more, you were chosen by God, who is love, to parent and help your child discover their gifts and purpose. You might even redefine who you are at the same time.

—✺—

One of the redefinitions for me has been writing and speaking about our experience. When Reid was eighteen, the Songstream Project invited us to participate in "Voices of Autism," their audio documentary featuring four families sharing how music had affected the lives of their teens with autism. I am forever grateful that they created a trustworthy, safe, intimate space for us to tell our story. Within it, I heard my husband say things for the first time that reframed events from our past. Maya Angelou wrote, "There is no agony like bearing an untold story inside of you." It is painful to imagine the loneliness of a world where no one knows your story. The relief of telling our stories enables just the opposite: connection and community, which are two primary gifts our children received from music. Almost magically, music made it possible for them to tell their stories, connect, and belong.

On the heels of that project, I presented with Talia Morales, a music therapist on the Songstream Project team, at an autism conference in Utah. Our aim was to move autism awareness beyond statistics to show how story and song, as well as music and memory, are intertwined. "Statistics don't move people, stories do," is one of their mottos.

Though it went famously in the end, I was nervous beforehand. My visionary and supportive husband inquired about it often, listened to me practice, and ensured my PowerPoint slides met his high standards from the advertising industry. His response after my first feeble delivery in our living room with the laptop teetering on the curved arm of our love seat was, "It feels like a book." He was right again.

So here it is, a book of specific examples from our son's life of how we leveraged his special interest in music to help him find purpose. As it was happening, we weren't necessarily sure what we were doing was right or wrong. Sometimes, in fact, Reid took the reins himself, and we hung on for dear life. We look back now, as if through a rearview mirror, and can distinguish a set of principles that helped us help him. Reid's special interest is in music and movies. We are grateful for the profession of music therapy that offered protocols to support his passion. On one hand, this book is the story of his life of music therapy. At the same time, it offers a sequence of ways you can discover your child's special interest and make it therapeutic, even if it is not music. I believe these principles are transferrable to help amplify other special interests, whether your child is obsessed with soccer, ballpoint pens, or garage door openers.

By distilling specific examples from Reid's life into a list of concepts, my hope is that each chapter will give you practical ideas that will immediately benefit you and your child. Each chapter begins with an accompanying music metaphor to expand your understanding of that principle, help you remember it, and motivate you to apply it in your own way. I share the concepts in loosely chronological order from birth through age twenty-one, so you can dip in and out as they are relevant to your journey. Remember, we didn't realize what we were doing at the time; only now can we name the threads that all wove together. Sometimes this process of looking back through the rearview mirror—whether mine or yours—enables us to move forward with new understanding and meaning.

I encourage you to read this book with a friend, your spouse, or another parent who can be a sounding board, help you apply the practical steps, and take action to move your child forward inch by inch. I would consider it a privilege to connect with you, hear your story, and brainstorm with you, too. Please feel invited to contact me on Facebook (Andrea Moriarty, Author) or by e-mail: andreamoriarty@mac.com.

# 1

*Sight-Read a New Piece*

## Study Your Child

## Sight-Read a New Piece

*Sight-reading is the musician's ability to play written music for the first time without practicing, specifically when the performer has not seen it before. It is also called a* prima vista.

*Meeting a baby in the hospital is like sight-reading a new piece. Rather suddenly in our case, we were interacting intimately with God's latest handiwork. Sight unseen, we had to figure out who these babies were and get acquainted. Without any rehearsal, so to speak, we were parents. It would require studying a child as if they were a fresh composition: previewing; scanning; anticipating; keeping our eyes on every note, bar, and phrase; following the notations of the composer.*

# 1

## Study Your Child

*I was born with music inside me. Music was one of my parts. Like my ribs, my kidneys, my liver, my heart. Like my blood. It was a force already within me when I arrived on the scene.*

—RAY CHARLES

Our story begins with adoption and an adrenaline rush that lasted the better part of a year. After being married seven years, with two weeks' notice, we adopted newborn twins, a boy and a girl. We felt elated and rewarded for having endured the helplessness of infertility. Having children through adoption turned out to be a leg up for us in terms of the first principle: to study your child. We couldn't assume either of these two precious babies would be at all similar to us. They were more likely *not* to have our curly hair or the same personality as Jim or me. We would have to study Reid and Allie to figure out who they were, how they were made, and what made them tick. The extended period of yearning to have a baby, then waiting for an adoption match, primed us to do it wholeheartedly. We weren't taking anything for granted.

I remember sitting for hours at the Neonatal Intensive Care Unit (NICU) and at home, staring into their eyes, asking God for wisdom in prayer, and observing them carefully to determine whether they were introverted, extroverted, neat and tidy, messy, structured, spontaneous, creative or conformist, interpersonal or independent. It was an intentional effort of noticing.

Jim remembers the attentive nurses taking pictures of baby Reid, whom we nicknamed "lobster man," saying, "We've never seen a baby do that." Such was his intensity, red all over, arching his back and wailing to high heaven like a mad hornet. That might have been our first clue that he was going to be different. Jim also remembers the nurses whispering, "Do you want to hold your baby girl now? She hasn't opened her eyes yet." That may have been when they bonded, their crystal blue eyes pooling into one as Jim took baby Allie in his arms.

My mom remembers my slightly neurotic, bossy directives to her (and any other helpers) that were really aimed at this getting-to-know-you effort of bonding: no excessive talking in the nursery, make eye contact during bottle feeding, play this lullaby cassette at naptime, and a list of other detailed instructions she had never considered when my brother or I were born.

There were many early indicators that Reid was sensitive to sound. As a preemie in the NICU, the various beeping and buzzing monitors startled him to no end. Every newborn reflex that professionals would check and identify for us later, we had seen before. His arms and legs jerked in staccato as if he were a conductor using all his limbs to signal a big finish. He was electric. The baby book we selected for him had a Keith Haring design on the cover that we thought resembled him; a graffiti-like, pop-art baby in bold primary colors was punctuated by black slash lines to indicate movement. Standing by his isolette caressing his tiny arms, I wondered if all the apparatuses stuck to him and connected to a red light or printout were really necessary. They stressed me out. When they alarmed I asked, "What do those mean? Is something wrong?" The nurses would calmly say, "Just put him back in for a bit. He's overstimulated." In her incubator around the corner, Allie looked as if she were catching up on her sleep.

As an infant, Reid didn't nap on garbage day because the rumbling of the truck and banging of the steel Dumpster lid would wake him. As a toddler, he didn't nap at all. I told babysitters if Reid was crying, he was overstimulated; if Allie was fussy, she was bored. Watching twins was a challenge for one sitter, all the more so if they were crying, wet, or hungry at the same time. My notes were intended to shortcut the troubleshooting and ensure harmony for all parties. I knew how upset Reid got if anyone smothered him with "goo goos" and "gaa gaas." Allie, on the other hand, would appreciate that and gurgle back. Little did I know how those notes would resemble the data we would compile years later to create a Behavior Support Plan[1] (BSP) for Reid. It turned out to be good practice. I was spelling out my mother's intuition ad infinitum so that family, babysitters, and, later, teachers and aides would know his triggers, preferences, and cues.

As sensitive as his ears were, it's a wonder his own screaming didn't bother him. It was unbearable to me, especially in the dark of night. Weaning him off a bottle and transitioning to sleep through the night were excruciating. I sat at the same place on our carpeted stair landing where I had cried my eyes out begging God for a child, now pleading with Him to calm this child or tell me what was wrong. My mom offered her stalwart support, saying,

---

1 A Behavior Support Plan is a plan that assists a student in building positive behaviors to replace or reduce a challenging or dangerous behavior. It includes teaching, improving communication, increasing relationships, and using clinical interventions.

"You can do it, Andrea. He has to cry it out. Don't go in there." We clocked the long minutes on my watch. Rather than wearing himself down, he escalated as if to a red line marked "terror," and I couldn't stand it any longer. I went in to hold him and join in the all-consuming emotion.

Even though we had an internal control group in our own nursery, the first pediatrician didn't listen to my concerns about Reid. "Oh, you're just comparing a boy and a girl," he said dismissively.

Allie slept well, ate well, napped, met all her milestones with ease, put single words together, smiled, cooed, held a crayon, and otherwise, made us look like we were doing everything right. Reid, on the other hand, quickly established his need for special handling with the church nursery staff, neighbors, and friends. He ended up in the bushes at play dates, seeking solace from the sand, slides, and erratic toddlers while Allie interacted with little-while friends and adults alike. She made everything look easy; he struggled to feel comfortable in his skin.

We learned to accept invitations tentatively and the fact that we might have to leave restaurants and parties quickly. The buzz of friends socializing in a family room sounds innocuous enough, but it was cacophony to Reid. Faster than I could accept a beverage, I was in pursuit, following him to protect a shelf of CDs or prevent a closet full of board games and puzzle pieces from collapsing. Before the food was served, he would begin to unravel with signs and sounds of mounting displeasure, which was our cue for the Irish exit. The tension of monitoring his unpredictable, constant motion and keeping his environment calm was an emotional and physical workout that outweighed the benefits of going out at all. Even walking around the block seemed impossible in seasons, because Reid was tempted to walk into every house to check their video collections.

His hypersensitivity to sound was most dramatic one night when we were out for dinner. A popular local pizza place offers arcade games in the back, surf movies playing in all four corners, and happy throngs of people imbibing microbrew. We had barely situated the two booster seats and slid Allie and Reid into them before Reid went off like a siren, screaming bloody murder. In an effort to be polite, I scooped him up and stepped outside on the sidewalk. Total silence. *Eh?* Back in we went for our pepperoni pie. After a repeat of the charade, even a new parent could figure it out. The chaotic mix of multiple inputs, background and foreground noise, was physically painful to him.

Gradually, over years he has learned to cover his ears, advocate not to go certain places, wear earphones, or brace himself for noise. And so have we. I give him advance notice before I flip on the blender. Jim warns him before turning on an electric drill. "I've got four more screws, buddy." One morning I wasn't aware of the construction going on at our neighbors' house across the street until I heard Reid standing on our stoop calling cordially to them. "Hello workers! You're doing a good job." He hears power tools, leaf blowers, ice cream trucks, and barking dogs from a mile away, literally.

One time when the kids were not yet two years old, we sat in the balcony of our church for a Christmas concert. Likely, we arrived a smidge late and that was the least obtrusive place to sneak in and find a seat, not to mention slip out early if need be. Just as I stopped panting and tuned into the program, I sensed Reid's distress in my lap. He was often wiggly; I'd been cracked in the chin more than a few times by his head swinging upward. This time elicited my curiosity, though; it was different. He was sobbing. I had no idea why. *Is he hurt? Did I pinch him? The music is not that loud. Does he object to being in the balcony? What is affecting him so strongly?*

Comforting and quieting his audible sobs, I looked over at Jim then down at the program to see the name of the song:

"Something-or-other in B Minor." It was a decidedly sad, instrumental song akin to "Mary Did You Know?" the heart-wrenching one about Jesus on the cross. We put it together; he was feeling the music that deeply. The minor key moved him to tears. We would see this repeated over time at other live performances, on the radio, and in his piano lessons. For him, the chords of a minor key were unbearable; he couldn't bring himself to play them. Of course, Reid didn't articulate this, but rather demonstrated unmistakable resistance through his behavior—getting up, leaving the area, blocking the teacher's hands, saying, "No, not that one," until we decoded the reason and he confirmed it heartily.

—⌒

Our pastor, Mark Foreman, describes parents as "anthropologists to these aboriginals running around in your house." Parents have about twenty years to get down on their level, learn their language and customs, and love them in their world. After all, that is exactly what God did for us. He gave incarnational love by sending His only son Jesus, to move among us and model victorious living in all its paradox. In their book, *Never Say No*, Mark and Jan Foreman reflect on raising their boys who are now key members of the alternative rock band, Switchfoot. "We do not create their unique natural gifts, but we can help our kids discover and polish these talents."

As children develop, the research phase of studying them gets easier and more obvious. Eventually, teachers help confirm or deny what we have already sensed in our guts; they give myriad assessments and evaluations to quantify it. Twenty years later, it is clearer than ever that the seeds of personality were intact from conception. Allie is introverted, organized, loves symmetry and coming alongside to help and include. Reid is extroverted, impulsive, loves to entertain, be in charge, and direct. They are both musically talented. The adoption letter we wrote as an appeal to birthparents mentioned music—my whistling in the kitchen and Jim's 750 GB hard drive of tunes. Maybe Allie and Reid's birthmother picked up on that when she chose us or maybe only God knew.

Studying your child can begin in utero and continues as you observe them at length with others, alone, in new settings, and in various life circumstances. It is an important first step toward identifying their strengths, temperament, needs, dreams, and special interests that might be a key to their future. Make an intentional effort to be a student of your child, noticing their likes and dislikes, appreciating how they learn, identifying how they are unique, and investigating what makes them come alive.

The questions at the end of each chapter are for you to think about, talk through with someone else who loves your child, and answer, in writing on paper. If you do that diligently, by the end of the book you will have a journal of sorts that will reveal patterns, next steps, and an action plan for you and your child. I encourage you to do this with a friend, a teacher, or your spouse as a deliberate way to study your child and discover their unique purpose. It will make the principles in this book more applicable and personal for you and your unique journey.

*What are some early core memories you have of your child?*

*What is something that has made them unique from an early age?*

*Is there some gift, attribute, or trait they seem to have been born with?*

# 2

*Connect with Your Audience*

## Notice What Others Notice

## Connect with Your Audience

*Performers connect with their audience during a concert as well as beforehand and afterward to create fans, build bonds, and make listeners want to help them. Once a connection is formed, fans will tell others about the artist, buy their music, merchandise, and tickets to their shows. If the connection is strong enough, listeners will never forget the performance, the music, or the artist. Jeff Tweedy, lead singer of Wilco, says, "Treating your audience like thieves is absurd. Anyone who chooses to listen to our music becomes a collaborator."*

*When you're facing an uphill battle and navigating uncharted waters with a challenging child, a few collaborators can come in handy. I used to chuckle at the mention that it takes a village to raise a child. Truth be told, you need a metropolis for some kids. We don't parent in a vacuum. Connecting with our audience, as parents, means being part of the village, enlisting helpful input from others, and being open to the objectivity of extended family, neighbors, and friends who care for and interact with our children. We don't aim to please them, but rather stay open and discerning to their input.*

# 2

## Notice What Others Notice

*Sometimes a person we love through no fault of his own,
can't see past the end of his nose.*

—MARY POPPINS

In addition to studying your child, it is important to notice—even ask, if you're that brave—what friends, family, and neighbors observe about him. In the moment, it may not be what you want to hear; people can be both wrong and cruel. However, if we are discerning and receptive, constructive input from an objective source can confirm a gut feeling and enhance our journey. Many wise parents, grandparents, and professionals have walked this road before us. Why not invite their invaluable insight?

I have had many a passerby lob unhelpful, derogatory comments in my general direction like, "You have your hands full," or, "You should teach your kid some manners," and even, "If you can't control him, I will." I rebuffed them silently in my head. *"Right, both hands,"* or, *"I'll add it to the long list,"* and, *"That might lead to a lawsuit."* People's ignorance, nosiness, and impertinence angered me. My instinct was to mouth off under my breath. My father-in-law heard me once and corrected, "Andrea, you can't expect them to know any better. They have no reason to know what you've learned. You can't blame them for that."

He was right. Looking back on it, I think we have a few options besides angry sarcasm when we feel like everyone is pointing fingers, but no one is throwing a rope. We can ignore them and focus on the positive. There will always be vultures and doves. Vultures feed on trash, dead meat, and thrive in dumps. Doves are strict vegetarians, thriving on seeds, never touching insects, and symbolizing peace. I think of them when I hear unhelpful comments and simply make a choice whether to taste it or chuck it. Will I be a vulture or a dove? What words from other people are worth eating?

Another option is to educate, although not everyone needs an explanation. I didn't feel we needed to explain anything to a cluster of beachgoers when Reid ran down the beach naked at four years old, but when he bolted from a public pool in his birthday suit at eight, I had some talking to do.

"Are you his mother? Where were you?" came with immediacy from an officer who pulled his squad car over at the busy intersection.

"Yes, yes! I'm here. Thank you," I sputtered, shaking from fright when I caught up to him. "I was in the girls' locker room with my daughter..." *And I need to go get her where I left her in the dust at that bus stop when I saw your flashers and came running.*

If someone is genuinely interested and I might see them again, I find a way to give them some facts they hadn't considered. It can be as simple as, "Reid has personal space issues." Or, "People with autism take things literally, so he did exactly what you said." They don't need to borrow any of my books to learn something new. One new fact might be enough. There were times I was tempted to snap back with self-righteous platitudes like, "He's a blessing," and too many times, I just rolled my eyes in disgust. My mom suggested I respond to unsolicited comments in the grocery store with a plea for help: "You can pray for us." But I never did that. I already had the whole church prayer chain—people I actually knew—praying for us.

We can give the dirty look, pass out one of those "My child has autism" cards,[2] or just share a knowing smile. That might be my personal favorite now that most of our community recognizes Reid. The knowing smile can say, "Don't worry," "I'm with him," "He means well," "We'll work on that next time," "Sorry 'bout that," and "Thank you for your grace," all in one fell swoop. Over time, I have determined that I don't need to apologize for Reid as much as interpret his behavior for the uninitiated. His actions aren't immoral or wrong; they just get misconstrued or misinterpreted. A simple explanation is usually all that is required, either to him or the puzzled onlooker. Like a sign language interpreter, I can give a simple gesture or few words that are all the explanation needed to change their attitude. Sometimes someone else does it for me. I see the lifeguards at our pool murmuring to one another in code words when Reid jumps in the shallow end or peels off the Velcro handrail cover. We've all learned to major on the majors and give grace freely.

Aside from the general public, whose comments must be sorted and sifted carefully, trusted friends will have valuable insight and can add unbiased wisdom to your perception of your own child. The part-time nanny who helped us until the kids were two was working on her speech and language pathology degree. She enrolled us in a San Diego State University research study that charted early language acquisition. She was also the first to suggest

---

2 Talk About Curing Autism (TACA) sells inexpensive business cards that acknowledge a child's behavior and explain autism without having to say anything. Tacanow.org

that Reid might fit the parameters for Pervasive Developmental Disorder (PDD). I fired her shortly after that, but have forgiven her. Just kidding, but isn't that our knee-jerk reaction as moms protecting our kin from danger and any kind of criticism, no matter how well-intentioned it might be? It wasn't easy to hear that from her at the time, but looking back, I can see how it was a helpful stepping-stone to getting early diagnosis and intervention for Reid. She provided the astute observation that our first pediatrician lacked, despite the red flags I was raising at each well-baby checkup.

A veteran mother of twins came to visit me when Allie and Reid were just toddling. She laughed almost vengefully as I bounded up our stairs, two at a time, to get a diaper. "Why are you laughing," I called down to her.

"Oh, just wait. It gets worse when they can walk…then run."

She was right; they went in different directions, and with great urgency, in our case. How well she knew the lose-lose proposition of loving two little ones who want Mommy at the same time, or chasing them when they go in two different directions. Some days it felt humanly impossible. I remember feeling accomplished that I could use the toilet while holding one swaddled baby, crying or calm.

⎯⎯⎯

Noticing what impresses others about our children can be helpful in predicting their strengths and unique gifts, as well as their deficits. Many children with Autism Spectrum Disorder (ASD) show enhanced music processing and an innate and superior ability to identify and recall pitch. We had this pointed out by a piano salesman who may have been upselling me, but I don't think so. Reid and Allie skittered around countless piano legs and climbed over every bench in the showroom as the skillful, unassuming, gentleman sat and played beautiful jazz selections on each and every upright as if he were Ray Charles. Observing the family dynamic and noting our needs, he was the first to comment on Reid's perfect pitch. "You better buy this one. He won't abide the other one being played." Duly noted, we would have several other music teachers and piano tuners confirm Reid's gift, in time.

As a toddler, Reid memorized every song title and page number in *My First Hymnal*, a preschool songbook he still adores. We could quiz him asking, "What number is 'Peace Like a River'?"

He would answer, "Twenty-nine" with an implied "duh."

Or the other way around. "What song is on page fifty-five?"

He would shoot back, "I Know a Fount."

He knew the entire book as well as the track numbers and song titles of most of the CDs we played in the car. This was more than a fun parlor game to impress other people; it was a definite skill. Even if they are peculiar, problematic, or stereotypical, splinter skills *are* skills, worth tuning into and developing. They can offset the despair that comes from our inevitable overfocus on the twenty-odd areas in which a child may be lagging, rather than one or two in which they excel. As life happens and our heads bob below the surface of the water, meeting daily needs and fielding input from an ocean of professionals, a splinter skill can be a bell buoy in the open sea. It is worth swimming toward and grabbing on to for dear life.

Great skill can be revealed through annoying, perseverative habits. Between the ages of two and five, (ahem, maybe seven) Reid had a penchant for peeling stickers that we didn't think would ever dissipate. Stickers presented themselves everywhere we went: parking lots, libraries, grocery stores. What were they covering? He had to know. Librarians seem to insist upon reinforcing the spine, labeling the genre, and color-coding every surface of their materials with stickers and gummy tape. Reid was compelled even more so to scrape them off to reveal the copyright year and fine print on every single item he mentally inventoried. How dare they deface such salient details?

While we didn't need others to point it out, his compulsion was undeniably noticeable. He discovered the stickiest of all stickers were license plate annual tags. Picking them off the neighbors' vehicles was pure satisfaction and could not be resisted. They beckoned from every driveway. As you might imagine, it was difficult to control this urge in parking lots. He would wander off and return, handing us a metallic bit with "FEB" or "97" on it. The unspoken, impossible challenge was to return it to the right vehicle. In the grocery stores at that time, you may not have noticed, but every item on every shelf was marked with an adhesive price label. They made shopping and staying in the cart unreasonable in Reid's mind. *He. Had. To. Peel. Them.* While it tried our patience, created a nuisance everywhere we went, and generally drove us crazy, it also represented a skill set in which Reid excelled. He was superior at pattern recognition, visual discrimination, memory, and persistence, all of which could be channeled into something useful.

Reid attended an inclusive, typical preschool program at a local church, while I homeschooled Allie for kindergarten. The first year, it went famously well. He had a wonderfully flexible teacher who kept a guitar strapped around her body and sang much of the day. He adored her and hung on her every melodic instruction. I'm pretty sure she added extra circle times to the daily routine like an Italian momma doling out helpings of tagliatelle and meatballs for the pure pleasure of fattening up her offspring.

The second year Reid was placed with an experienced teacher in the next room. How can I put this? As long as she was unwilling to use music, "preschool" as it is commonly known, was not happening. She was a firm, no-nonsense woman with no laugh lines. Her classroom was abuzz with activity stations. Clusters of preschoolers busied themselves stacking blocks, gluing tissue-paper crafts, and building forts underneath a bunk bed loft, all at the same time. The auditory onslaught was significant even before a wooden block tower inevitably toppled or bins full of plastic kitchen utensils rattled onto the linoleum floor. More than twenty children and a handful of adults bounced from one conversation to the next, commenting and kibitzing with no central focus.

It was a long year of reassigning Reid's one-on-one aide, increasing visual supports, negotiating modifications, and trying to be nice. We might have done better to offer the teacher guitar lessons. With music, Reid could attend and participate happily. Without it, he was off to the side dismantling bulletin boards, dumping dry kidney beans, or slipping out the side door to run water in the adjacent restroom sinks. Without any unifying order, I imagine he figured the goal was to add to the chaos. Everyone noticed this: the only preschool classroom that worked for Reid was the one with the guitar-wielding, musical teacher. If she was absent, not to mention when she retired, his attention was lost. Whether or not they took it personally, Reid's clear preference impressed all the staff. (Was it really a preference, or a need for the music in order to cope and concentrate?) It was another early indicator of his special interest as well as what kind of classroom he would require.

Another undeniable trait others helped me recognize in Reid was his love of people, albeit one at a time if he had his preference.

Defying his diagnosis in a sense, therapist after therapist would comment, "Reid makes me feel like the most important person in the world." As they entered the revolving door of our house to implement his home program, Reid rolled out a virtual red carpet, bellowing the first and last name of the new arrival, flinging his arms like a conductor letting loose fireworks, and leaping onto our living room love seat to absorb the impact of his uncontainable glee. He did this to welcome "Janelle Scott!" and "Carla Wood!" and "Sarah Fields!" bestowing each of them with celebrity status. No matter how difficult their session might be, whether he kicked, screamed, or ignored them, he had a charismatic ability to win others over. They might leave in a sweat after he ran them ragged around an imaginary mulberry bush, resisted oral motor exercises, upset buckets of toy figurines, and wriggled away from directives like a little greased piglet, but he was still their favorite.

Even the bohemian doctor in Berkeley, CA, who diagnosed Reid with autism at age three, delivered the rather grim label with a hopeful note. She worked with a partner in a team approach, leaving the dirty work of outlining Reid's deficits and the impossibility of my situation to a young assistant. Saving the best for last, she cocooned us in her book-lined nook. Leaning on the edge of her swivel chair, she locked eyes with me in maternal solidarity to share her bit. "This is a kid who loves words. He loves the sound of them in his ears and the feel of them tripping off his tongue." I loved her for seeing the gift in him.

Invite and listen to the impressions of people who interact with your child to help you discover who they are, how they learn, what motivates them, and where they excel. This outside input can help you envision who they are becoming and know how to guide them. Noticing what impresses others about your child will encourage you on the long days and help you foster the strengths and special interests that may become their purpose in life. At the same time, be discerning about whether to respond or dismiss comments that are just hurtful and mean. You may be modeling a life skill your child will need in years to come to defend and advocate for himself.

*What compliments do you hold dear about your child?*

*What do other people notice about your child?*

*What stands out or impresses people about your child?*

# 3

*Appreciate the Minor Keys*

Embrace Differences

## Appreciate the Minor Keys

*Notes on a major scale sound bright and cheerful while notes on the minor scales are more solemn, melancholy, or sad. Minor scales provide a change in scenery from their major counterparts and are more interrelated than you might think.*

*In life, as well as music, the ups and downs punctuate one another. Expectations and pinnacle moments meld with disappointments and loss to give us a full range of experiences and empathy with others. Our diversity as individuals also adds texture and interest to life. If we were all the same, life would be as monotonous as a piece of music in one octave, with just three notes, or just white keys.*

*To celebrate the completion of their documentary, the Songstream Project threw an experiential listening party. That night, music therapist Vanessa Contopulos debuted a song she wrote after hearing the nuances of our story. She truly believes "Everyone's story is worth telling and every story is worthy of a song." The lyrics of "Unexpected Ways," describe this correlation between life and the minor keys.*

*I remember when we got the letter for the first time*
*I knew our lives would be intertwined*
*Because you were meant for me*
*You are here to help me see*
*And I've come to love the minor keys*

*They are the rain that makes the hills so green*
*And longer is better it seems when it comes to you and me*
*Gives me time to see*
*The unexpected ways your joy is changing me*

# 3

## Embrace Differences

*Disability is a natural part of the human experience that does not diminish the right of individuals with developmental disabilities to enjoy the opportunity to live independently, enjoy self-determination, make choices, contribute to society, and experience full integration and inclusion in the economic, political, social, cultural, and educational mainstream of American society.*

—THE DEVELOPMENTAL DISABILITIES ASSISTANCE
AND BILL OF RIGHTS ACT

A diagnosis can slam the breaks on parents' dreams. While it actually doesn't change anything about our children, it changes how the world perceives them. Letting go of expectations is an important part of the parenting process, especially when special needs are involved. We can only dream new dreams if we do. Once we accept that the journey will not be whatever efficient beeline we envisioned, and that the destination may even change, we can enjoy a more scenic route to a place where our children belong, and so do we.

The most damaging thing a diagnosis threatens to do is to kill our hope that our child will amount to anything. There is an inherent danger if we project that onto their growing self-esteem. Itemizing the delays and deficits is a necessary evil in order to reach a diagnosis, but it is disheartening at best. I felt defeated sitting in a consult room with Allie in my lap, listening with me to a team of professionals describe the results of their assessments of her brother. "So, these activities you do at home, you say Allie will do them with you and it takes longer for Reid. How much longer, would you say?" Reid tried to pull the pegs out of a hammer and nail block toy as if he wasn't listening, but of course, he absorbed every word.

"Umm...maybe a couple weeks," I guesstimated not to incriminate Reid. For me, the very question set up a comparison between my two children that was accurate, yet set an unfair and potentially unhealthy precedent. I loved them both; they were just different! It was Mark Twain who wrote, "Comparison is the death of joy."

At age two Allie had a typical lexicon of one hundred words she could link into sentences; Reid had a handful of words he used one at a time. Allie wanted and played with friends; Reid wasn't interested in other kids unless they had something he wanted. Allie adjusted to new settings; Reid resisted a change in the wind direction. Allie could write her name and do coloring; Reid couldn't hold a pencil. Reid would continue to lag far behind Allie in terms of measurable benchmarks, yet to this day he has not plateaued in making progress. I used to take heart reading *Leo the Late Bloomer*, but even that needs a sequel.

As late as ten years old, teachers and occupational therapists advised us to teach Reid to type on an AlphaSmart device because he was so resistant to handwriting. They'd nearly given up after investing hours of time correcting his prehensile grasp. Yet one day when we least expected it, a brand-new teacher presented him with an alternative way to hold a pencil "that might be more comfortable." He decided to do it and now writes copious lists of television episodes for the sheer pleasure of it. Her belief in him seemed to make the difference. She didn't allow labels to hinder possibility.

———⌇———

Reducing the diagnosis to a menial tool that would allow insurance to continue covering speech and occupational therapy, helped us keep perspective and downplay its hold on us. In reality, it ends up providing more perks than we asked for or imagined. It has redefined who we are, opened doors to new understanding, and given us full access to the wonders of the natural world. Literally, we got to explore the Grand Canyon without the crowds thanks to Reid's diagnosis. With his Lifelong Disability Pass from the National Parks Service, we drove right through a barricaded "Do Not Enter" gate while throngs of tourists waved their hands, flagging us to, "Stop! You can't go there." *Oh, yes we can*, I thought as I got out and entered the four-digit code they'd given us. *Watch me!* That day we celebrated the privilege we'd been given. But that wasn't always the case.

I well recall the whiplash and careening that ensued when I realized the autism shoe fit Reid. Like a traumatic car crash, life went into slow-motion and wouldn't stop replaying. The reverse-Cinderella story felt like a bait-and-switch curse on the blessing of twins we had received. I didn't want these crystal slippers. For nights on end, I bawled my eyes out, alone on the sofa in the family room of our new house. Once the kids were asleep, I watched borrowed library videos on autism and recognized the symptoms all too well. Jim was gone Monday through Friday on an even more exciting business venture than the one that had landed us in a stately historic property just outside the Windy City. I was new in town, new at church, and new to the Easter Seals Disability Services center. My mom had just remarried at fifty-eight and was behaving more like a newlywed than a grandmother. She was giddy, distracted, and basically as elated as I was devastated. It was miserable timing; I was alone with a capital A.

While I had been excited to return to our Midwestern roots, be within driving distance of our families, and enjoy the wraparound porch and no fences separating us from the friendly neighbors, Chicago became synonymous with diagnosis, abandonment, and anger in my memory and our family lexicon. It was either frigidly cold or swelteringly hot. To make matters worse for Jim, there was no surf. He literally met our neighbors for the first time at a block party the following spring when he announced we were putting the house on the market.

"Hello, name's Jim, great to meet you."

"How's the house?"

"Um, well, we're selling it and moving back to California."

We relocated every October for three years as he kept pace with the height of the dot-com startup era. Moving to San Francisco from Chicago felt like we were leaving the scene of a crime. Those first evaluations by total strangers were painful. Inviting social workers into your home from the local school district only to have them itemize the ways your child falls short was the antithesis of Welcome Wagon. Allie and I became a team in and out of the fishbowl. We traipsed around to Reid's new appointments three times a week, talking, coloring, and playing games while we watched him in therapy through the two-way glass.

Jim trusted me implicitly to manage the house, the finances, the kids, and our social calendar while he gave his all at work. It was a good arrangement for the most part. But right then, I didn't want his trust so much as I wanted him to share the emotional burden. When he didn't, I got mad at him, my mom, and God. Especially God, because the buck stopped with Him. How could He do this to me? I felt duped. He was ultimately responsible. After giving us twins, He was pulling a fast one to let one have a-a-au—that unmentionable word. Anger, denial, bargaining, it was all there, the steps of the grieving process without any of the redemption that would come from seeing a bigger picture. Each night, I would wallow in the frozen muck and wake with my tears turned to icicles.

The more I sobbed, the more obvious it became. If I stayed mad at God I would really have no one. To alienate myself from the One who had the answers and created these kids would be shooting myself in the foot. 2 Chronicles 15 says, "The Lord is with you when you are with him. If you seek him, he will be found by you, but if you forsake him, he will forsake you." I remember a moment in the living room of that house when I turned off one of the depressing autism documentaries and had the epiphany: this could be worse. The devastating prognosis that I wished would go away was going to be hard. I wouldn't be able to do it alone. My usual support system was absent. How would I manage this?

Perhaps the deeper question I wasn't even muttering was: *Who could I blame?* I had not signed up for this. I did not see it coming. I was not equipped. And I did not like it. Somewhere in that swirl of negative emotions I realized that to stay mad at God would be to refuse His help. I'd been stubborn before about blocking people out of my life and that was hard work too. If I turned my back on God in bitterness, I would really be all alone. Ugly hints of anger, blame, self-pity, bitterness, and fear bubbled up into a whiff of methane or carbon dioxide. I knew it would kill me to stay in that unclean spot. To survive I would need to move to cleaner air and keep talking to God, if only to communicate my dissatisfaction. At the very least, He was listening to me rant. All alone in that big house after dark, I needed someone to tell my problems to and at the moment He seemed like the only candidate.

It wasn't quite a bolt of lightning, nor did the Mother Abess from *The Sound of Music* appear to encourage me with Psalm 121 as I set out to cross the Alps, on foot. "Remember: 'I lift mine eyes unto the hills from whence cometh my help." But in that moment I decided that I needed God's help more than I needed someone to blame. My head nodded awake from the stupor and I began the long process of leaning in to understand what the Mother Abess' meant when she exhorted Maria "to live the life you were born to live."

The conundrum of possible treatments and interventions only underscored the fact that God alone was omniscient. I might need his counsel more than the guesswork that was spewing from specialists and experts. What did they really know anyway? They didn't know me. They didn't know our story. I wasn't even sure they knew my God. I succumbed and, in so many words, told God, *I might be stubborn, but I'm not stupid. I best not alienate you, God. I don't like this, but I won't force you out. I need your help.*

I wouldn't have faced that reality so squarely had Jim or my mom been more present in those months. From studying the Old Testament, I have learned there is no word for coincidence in Hebrew. So in a melancholy way, Chicago was a blessing. God would sustain all of us long past the circumstances of my mom's new wedding or Jim's latest career move. Years later I would internalize what Beth Moore[3] puts so well in her *Living Free: Learning to Pray God's Word* Bible study: "We naturally think if God answers a prayer or grants a miraculous healing, it is because He loves us.

---

3 Beth Moore has numerous Bible studies available as workbooks and DVD series.

If we pray and the answer is no, we question God's love. But beloved, healing or answered prayer has absolutely nothing to do with whether He loves you. It has to do with God's purposes and plans for your life."

———

When Reid was still a preschooler, we had a peculiar experience at Cedar Point amusement park in Sandusky, Ohio, where we went for an extended family reunion. They have a karaoke attraction where kids can sing along with the Peanuts characters. Reid took a shortcut to the center-stage microphone, uninhibited by anyone or anything. He didn't wait in lines at that point. As a matter of fact, he still doesn't. (I just left an Individualized Education Plan (IEP)[4] meeting where I agreed to make "waiting in line in the community" one of his goals at age twenty-one.)

Unconcerned with the legality of a proper queue, a theme park employee in disc jockey garb took requests from the small children as they sang their favorite songs with Snoopy, Lucy, and Linus characters. Reid's first request: "Tis a Gift to be Simple," the Shaker folk hymn. They didn't have that one. Nor the next three songs he asked for. I think he settled for the "Happy Birthday" song, since it was the only intersection of his tastes and their options. My point here is that atypical is OK. We don't all have to sing the same songs.

When Reid was a preteen, a teacher friend of the family made a passing comment that follows me like an echo wanting an answer. Reid, bless his heart, was conspicuous in many places: at church, the grocery store, their house, even the park. He jumped lines, invaded

---

4 An Individualized Education Plan (IEP) is a legally binding document meant to address each child's unique learning issues and include specific educational goals. The federal Individuals with Disabilities Education Act requires that public schools create an IEP for every child receiving special education services.

personal space norms, spoke a bit loudly, and bolted unexpectedly, all in a most delightful, contagious way. I suppose she had watched me in enough settings, trying to get him to comply, conform, or do whatever "right thing" would make him fit in at that particular venue. This particular time she said kindly, "You know, Reid is always gonna be Reid." Maybe that was when I began to stop myself from apologizing for his boldness, explaining his idiosyncrasy, and letting my hypervigilant correction preempt every social interaction. We had friends who knew what to expect, loved his enthusiasm, and were fine with it spilling over on them. Why wasn't I?

It was in church on Sundays that the gulf between correcting and accepting Reid's buoyant *"je ne sais quoi"* was most at odds. In the middle of the fourth-grade Sunday school curriculum, we deserted the children's ministry to keep Reid with us in the sanctuary. The consistency of the liturgy and a printed program trumped the auditory processing and cognitive demands of small group discussion with peers and a different volunteer facilitator each week.

We attended a Presbyterian church with pews; Reid might have fit in better at a Pentecostal revival tent. He would stand for all the songs, actually before the songs, as the band took their positions. He sang and danced along, then sat when the band sat and exited when the music was over. He worshipped with abandon, hands over his head, hips swaying, feet sashaying down and out of the constraining pew into the aisle. He was hard to miss, even though we staked a claim on the back row of the side transept as our regular spot. In good conscience, I couldn't make him sit down or keep "quiet hands" in his lap to lyrics like:

> *So we raise up holy hands*
> *To praise the Holy One*
> *Who was and is and is to come*

He was like the prophet Miriam, Aaron's sister, after the Israelites were safe across the Red Sea. In Exodus 15, she "took a timbrel in her hand and led them all with dancing," except no one was following him. Until the sermon started, it seemed like everyone else might do better to follow his lead. In fact, nine weeks out of ten, someone would come up to me at the end of the service and say, "We should all be more like your son," or, "Don't you wish you could be as free as he is?" or, "You know God must be so pleased watching him worship." Maybe the first couple folks were merely being polite, but as it continued I began to believe them.

Reid's atypical, exuberant behavior may not have blended in, but it did serve a purpose. He was blessing others. Far be it for me to stand in the way of that. It wouldn't be the first time God acted in ways opposite of what we expect. My most poignant memory was when an awkward, coerced spouse who joined his wife on occasion stopped me to say, "I am so glad that your son is here. I figure, if he can be here, so can I." As often as a voice inside my head would taunt, *I can't believe you bring him here. You should just stay home,* those around me would correct it and thank me for bringing him with comments like, "I love sitting in front of him and hearing his voice."

Oh, there were dirty looks and stares as well, but the well-wishers balanced them out. I learned to put blinders on to avoid the judgmental looks and focus instead on the positive. This was a mental discipline as much as a coping strategy. How else could I show my face again in public or get out of bed some mornings? Romans 12:2 calls it "renewing your mind" in order to be transformed rather than conform to the pattern of this world. First Corinthians 10 calls it taking "captive every thought to make it obedient to Christ." With practice, I learned to think new thoughts that agreed with God's Word. For starters, Reid was a blessing not a nuisance. He was a child of the King (Galatians 3:26) and God had prepared good works in advance for him to do (Ephesians 2:10). When I stayed fixed on what is true, noble, right, pure, lovely and of good repute (Philippians 4:8) rather than what was wrong, unfair, hurtful, or depressing, I felt better. As I consciously chose to let God's truth from the Bible supersede what I was hearing from culture and all around me, I could maintain a better attitude and more productive action. We always have a choice where our mind dwells and our behavior flows from there.

⟶ᦓ

Benjamin Zander, conductor of the Boston Philharmonic and their Youth Orchestra, has written an incredible book with his wife who is a family therapist. *The Art of Possibility* offers many examples of how he shifts paradigms to motivate his highly accomplished students to be more creative and achieve greatness. He writes, "In the measurement world, you set a goal and strive for it. In the universe of possibility, you set the context and let life unfold."

We would do well to integrate some of that special sauce in our families and educational system for those with and without disabilities. Goals are worth setting as long as they don't put a ceiling on possibilities, squash exuberance, or limit potential. His wife Rosamund goes on, "Every problem, every dilemma, every dead end we find ourselves facing, only appears unsolvable inside a particular frame or point of view. Enlarge the box, or create another frame around the data, and problems vanish, while new opportunities appear." I didn't discover their book and apply it to our situation until Reid was a teen, but it summarizes what I had strived to do his whole life. Against a rising tide of naysayers and realists, we were eternal optimists. This gave it credence; we were reframing our family life.

A paradoxical freedom can accompany a diagnosis, if we allow it. Remember in *Willy Wonka and the Chocolate Factory*, when the five lucky children enter the factory, and wacky Mr. Wonka has them sign that enormous contract on the wall? Most of the parents voice reasonable objections:

"I didn't know we had to sign anything for this tour."

"Don't talk to me about contracts, Wonka; I use 'em myself. They're strictly for suckers."

"Violet, baby, don't you sign anything there. I don't sign anything without my lawyer."

But not Grandpa Joe. He hasn't left their shabby apartment, or even his bed, in years. Embracing the risk he blurts out, "Sign away, Charlie, we got nothin' to lose!"

I heard this same sentiment from a youth worker as I debated the merits of Reid attending overnight camp. He listened to me express our fundamental fear as parents, "What if he fails?"

Then he countered with, "Hasn't he already failed?" In other words, what did he have to prove? With his diagnosis and needs, Reid would have a one-on-one aide, an explanation to give other campers for any missteps, and the outside chance of enjoying himself. There was no downside to risking it.

There is no such thing as failing when no one expects anything of you. Many of our students on the spectrum have no place to go but up. Reid has done so many things I never imagined, from distinguishing "yes" from "no," to writing his name, tying his shoes, flying to New York City and riding on subways. Integrating this concept of Embracing Differences gives our kids the freedom to learn at their own pace and in their own way. It gives them room to fail and to succeed. It requires holding things in a certain tension, accepting their diagnosis, learning all about it, while also letting go of expectations and opening up the possibility that they might defy that diagnosis in the name of individuality and the miraculous. Even very slow progress accumulates and you may find your kids are more like the tortoise than the hare. Celebrate who they are and their unique way of experiencing life.

*How is your child different than you expected?*

*Is there a dream for your child you need to let go of?*

*What new vision could you imagine of your child or for them?*

# 4

*Check for Sharps and Flats*

Look for the Affinity

## Check for Sharps and Flats

*In musical notation, a key signature is a group of sharp or flat symbols on the staff lines at the beginning of the piece. They designate which notes are to be played higher or lower than the natural notes. The key signature applies throughout the entire piece. Accidentals are notes that don't usually occur in the key the piece of music is in. Easy to spot, they will have a sharp ♯, natural ♮, or flat ♭ sign in front of them. An accidental is an exception to the key signature.*

*If genius is abnormality, then differences can't be all bad. While we are ticking off the major milestones our kids reach or wondering whether they are on track developmentally, it is important to also stay alert for accidentals. These sharps and flats, if you will, could be the spark of genius that begins as a special interest, affinity, or fascination. Don't be surprised if these exceptions appear at the expense of more typical skills.*

# 4

## Look for the Affinity

*Passion is one great force that unleashes creativity, because if you're passionate about something, then you're more willing to take risks.*

—Yo-Yo Ma

Identifying a child's special interest or passion—for music, sprinkler heads, or popcorn—can unlock a world of potential and change the course of their life. Sometimes it will be obvious, as it was with Reid's obsession with music and movies. If it doesn't present itself naturally, it is worth searching for like treasure, and then investing in it heavily. Go back over family memories, outings, conversations, and early photos, mining for little details that might add up to a pattern, a fascination, an affinity.

I readily relate to Mary in the Bible, because she knows what it is like to lose a child and "pondered so many things in her heart." At the very beginning when Jesus was born in less than ideal conditions, Mary, like so many mothers, pondered silently why and what it might mean. Then again when he was twelve, she pondered what he was doing when he was lost from the family caravan in the big city. For three days, they searched frantically until they found him in the temple, dialoguing with rabbis. Can you imagine? After three days we'd have helicopters and a Facebook campaign launched. Young Jesus's explanation to his parents in Luke 2 was simply, "Where did you think I would be? Didn't you know I would be in my Father's house?" His calling and affinity were so strong that he thought it would be obvious where to find him.

We lose Reid easily, and often. More times than I can count, he has gone missing at Target stores, farmers' markets, schoolyards, and malls. "Where's Reid?" is a recurrent call to action for us. Immediately, I pause and pray, *"Lord show us where he is and protect him until we get there."* Allie developed a system, not unlike the one in *Ian's Walk*, a picture book by Laurie Lears. One time when she was about seven, I asked her, "How do you always know where he is?"

She explained, "I close my eyes and think like Reid. I think if I were him, where would I be?" Inevitably, we find him one of three places: crouched in front of the nearest display of videos or electronics, at the foot of a stage where music is playing, or splashing in a water element.

Once at the Tate Modern in London, we lost him for more than twenty minutes. The fright of imagining how quickly he could scamper up the gaping ramp of their Turbine Hall, down the Bankside river walk, and across the Millennium Bridge caused us to enlist help from security quicker than usual. Art museums have surveillance cameras and two-way radios; this could be the best possible place to lose and find him. *This will be easy*, we thought. Instead, impish Reid at ten years old seemed to have evaded their monitors. This alarmed us even further. As the clock ticked, they could not spy him in any of the galleries. In the end, Allie's method proved superior when she spotted him on the carpeted floor of the gift shop just below the sightline of the cameras. He was innocently browsing their DVD selection.

As irresistible as Curious George, he silently acknowledged us as if to say, "What's all the fuss? I'm right here." I still remind him to take that extra step and just tell me where he's going.

As we think of our children, what are the things we ponder in our heart of hearts or wonder the meaning of? If your child goes somewhere without you, it might be a clue as to what he wants to pursue as a special interest. In those emotionally charged moments, they might be showing you their mission in life.

It was easy to see Reid's affinity for music on a family trip to Williamsburg. He kept pace with the fife and drum corps—and we trailed like hound dogs—for nearly an hour all the way down Duke of Gloucester Street to their final staging area on a side street behind a white picket fence. Their snare beats and whistling fifes called him like a Pied Piper, compelling him to pursue them. His body language screamed, "At last, someone who speaks my language!" He jumped gleefully like a self-activating pogo stick in the photo we took of him posing next to one of the summer-stock snare drummers. Donning his souvenir tricornered hat, Reid barely reached the young man's knees, but he was ablaze, eager to enlist.

⎯ᴄ⎯

In his book *Life, Animated*, Ron Suskind dubbed the term "affinity therapy" for the ways he and his wife entered into their son's obsession with Disney movies to engage him in the world, eventually in highly sophisticated ways. The response to his book was so great, he created the Autism Affinities Project online, where others are invited to submit examples of the passions that consume and motivate them. Everything from anime and wind chimes to football and dogs is documented there.

For Reid, much like their son Owen, music and movies were the clear affinity. Put them together into what is widely known as a movie musical; now, that's nirvana. Various movie scenes, especially those set to music, helped him communicate and understand the world. Like others we know, Reid would use snatches of movie scripts in apt ways to express his wants, deepest emotional needs, feelings, and understanding of the world. We were wise to do likewise, if we wanted to reach him.

This practice of memorizing scripts and calling them up when appropriate is common for kids on the spectrum. Speech therapists may refer to it at first as delayed echolalia, but moms know what their kids mean. It is not random or accidental; it's a code. One friend remembers her son, as a toddler of very few words, repeating, "Pooh Bear wants honey, Pooh Bear wants honey." In short order, she deciphered that he meant, "I'm hungry." If we study the videos and movies our children prefer, this affinity and code language becomes a way to engage with them. Walt Disney seemed to know this instinctively. "Movies can and do have tremendous influence in shaping young lives in the realm of entertainment towards the ideals and objectives of normal adulthood."

Often I remind Reid of the line from *Mary Poppins*, "The constable is respons-ta-ble, now how does that sound?" It works like a charm when it is time to take out the trash or clear his dinner plate from the table. When Jim is a little abrupt, reminding me of Mr. Banks, a simple, "George, you're always so forceful," mellows him right out. Before he leaves for a business trip, Jim harkens back to a scene from *Old Yeller* and tells Reid "while I'm gone, you'll be the man of the house." Drawing parallels to and from the shows Reid has committed to memory enables him to access life skills in a new context and effectively role-play. It also makes the habitual viewing serve him well after the movies are turned off.

Anna Vagin, PhD, has published two books, *Movie Time Social Learning* and *YouCue Feelings: Using Online Videos for Social Learning*, sharing how she used both full-length movies and YouTube shorts therapeutically with clients to teach social skills, language, and emotional intelligence. She offers fifty activities that develop emotional intelligence when used in conjunction with watching four-minute animations like "Ormie the Pig" or "On the Level." The movies become an accessible springboard for visual diagramming and application. I just discovered these and Reid, at twenty-one, can still learn a lot about reading situational cues, facial expressions, and abstract reasoning from them.

Other affinities can also be leveraged for learning and engagement. Reid has a peer whose passion is surfing. Every time he sees my husband, who is an avid surfer and worked in the industry, he greets him with, "Ya been surfing? How's the surf?" (Actually, he sounds just like most of our neighbors in Southern California.) From there, he launches into a weather report on the waves, details of various boards, and an update on his job at a local surf shop. When he reached transition age and completed high school, his parents capitalized on his interest in surfing by moving to a newly remodeled house with a separate egress so he would qualify for supported living. The new address was carefully chosen to be in walking distance from the surf shop where this young man continues to work and thrive in his element.

Another friend has a son who is obsessed with engines in general, and ambulances, specifically. No telling where that might lead; but for now, they regularly walk to the nearby hospital to watch emergency vehicles zoom in with sirens and flashers blaring. It generates conversation and engagement for him. Yet another of Reid's peers loves trains, so he and his mom ride the rails on weekends to different stations up and down the coast. So many extension lessons leap to mind from *The Boxcar Children* book series, to Walt Disney's Barn rail museum, to photographing all the conductors. Don't get me started.

At the Utah conference, a college student raised his hand at the end to ask me, "Could this be applied to people without autism?" I learned his story afterward at our table. He had struggled to sit still in grade school, doodled incessantly, and been chastised for it. He wished teachers had encouraged him to submit his assignments as graphic novels. Years later, he is pursuing a niche as a cartoonist so that he can do the very thing that he is good at and loves as a profession.

Paula Kluth, respected inclusion expert, explains, "If educators could reframe obsessions as fascinations, passions, interests, or enthusiasms and see them as potential tools, educators and their students may potentially be more satisfied, calm, and successful." Her book, *Just Give Him the Whale*, offers twenty ways to use these fascinations, or areas of expertise, to support students: to boost literacy, minimize anxiety, improve mathematics skills, teach manners, and encourage greatness, to name a few. "Interests can sometimes be limiting but they can also be freeing, calming, motivating, captivating, and inspiring."

—❦—

Through the lens of his passion for music, we were able to see how empathetic Reid is. Empathy is a commonly assumed deficit for those on the autism spectrum. Equally common is how music enables empathy and expression of feelings. Leo Tolstoy wrote, "Music is the shorthand of emotion." It is also an alternative way to demonstrate feelings if one cannot articulate them with words. Both Reid and Curtis, another participant in the "Voices of Autism" program, draw on a vast musical inventory to find specific songs to communicate their feelings. Songs help them show comprehension of an emotional situation as well as evoke and share a specific deep emotion. For Curtis, a selection from the *Lord of the Rings* theme moves him to tears, and has enabled him to understand sadness.

Days after our dog Benny died, we were driving home on Highway 5 in San Diego, unsure what to say or how to process the loss. In her senior year of high school, Allie would miss Benny the most, since he had slept on her bed and offered her undivided attention. Benny was a sturdy, barrel-chested lab mix who looked so much like Old Yeller we called him "New Yeller." He gave faithful assistance when we had to search for Reid in the neighborhood. Reid liked Benny as long as he didn't bark. His deep, protective bark set off a series of startle reflexes like dominos throughout our house. Reid would freeze in momentary paralysis, then burst into a panicked flight pattern, trying to recreate the offending disturbance by slamming doors, ringing the bell repeatedly, and sounding his own piercing scream at the top of his lungs. Adding to the mayhem, the additional doorbell sounds triggered Benny to bark again in a dreadful reprise. The frenzy was more absurd than the "Posts everyone!" scene in *Mary Poppins;* it subsided with Reid biting a pillow or sometimes his own arms. Needless to say, we did not look forward to unexpected visitors, or the UPS truck slowing at our curb.

Still, Benny was a great dog. It was unclear whether Reid understood that Benny was gone forever. He hadn't appeared to be tracking the process until he took a turn as deejay on my phone. We do this often as a family activity in the car, taking turns picking songs from my music app. This time, his choice conveyed both empathy and an uncanny comprehension of all that had happened. He cued up a version of "It is Well with my Soul," by Chris Rice, a bittersweet hymn of acceptance and closure that was played at my stepfather's memorial. It met the needs of the moment, comforting the rest of us and confirming Hans Christian Andersen's maxim that, "Where words fail, music speaks."

Reid took this code-mode of communication one step further when he watched video scenes repeatedly with intent. Over time, presuming competence[5] and studying him, I was able to decode the ways he was using them to tell me or show me something. His persistent rewinding and replaying of the same scene was a signal. Either something happened at school that he needed to process or he was working through a new concept.

For instance, when he was about twelve, he played "A King and His Hawk," an episode from *Between the Lions*, repeatedly and insistently. Watching it with him, I came to understand his remorse over an incident with a teacher. Through tears he told me, "That was Ms. Hirsch."

Once I understood, it worked both ways. I could think of scenes to teach him new abstract concepts. He loved the scene from *Air Bud*, when Buddy the dog has to choose which master he will serve: the mean clown who mistreats him or the kind boy, Josh Framm, who truly loves him. Using that image as a mental screen

---

5  To presume competence is best explained by Kathie Snow on her Disability is Natural website. When in doubt of how much someone with a disability understands, rather than risk condescending or insulting their intelligence, it is best to presume competence. It has a marked way of raising expectations, performance, and consciousness.

saver, I explained to him how we also get to choose whether to serve God as our master—He is loving and truly cares for us like Josh Framm—or follow the temptations of the enemy who is the father of lies and mistreatment, like the clown. I might also have mentioned Bob Dylan's lyric, "You're gonna have to serve somebody." He got it and would repeat it back to me.

Just the other day in his adult-transition program, Reid's teachers reported that he was distracted by a classmate who was blurting out vocalizations at the computer next to him. Once he stopped staring at her and settled into his own computer turn, he yelled, "The boy who cried wolf!" It's anyone's guess whether that was off-topic or an apt commentary on the girl's behavior based on his understanding of the idiom from another episode of "Between the Lions." I wasn't there, but the latter wouldn't surprise me.

Reid's interest in *Mary Poppins* lasted the longest, bordering on obsession. For more than a decade, all roads led to *Mary Poppins*. The movie became a metaphor of great proportions during his adolescence when a real-life Mary Poppins showed up on our doorstep and seemed to be God's agent to carry our family through the difficult season and turn everything upside down. After three years, she left as quickly as she came, yet I can correlate every single scene selection of the movie with a spiritual lesson she helped us see.

Like the scene where Jane and Michael Banks take a peek up the chimney shaft, our kid's self-absorption in a limited topic can seem at first like "it's awfully dark and gloomy up there." Let Bert the chimney sweep set you straight. "There now. You see how wrong people can be? That there is what you might call a doorway to a place of enchantment." If we are alert like Bert was at every dark corner on the *Mary Poppins* set, we will look for our child's affinity and enter into it with them. Kristine Barnett, who wrote *The Spark*, was not content to believe the professionals' dire prognosis for her young son who stared for hours on end, fascinated by shadows on the wall. Instead, she invested herself in whatever he could do and maximized it. He turned out to have a higher IQ than Einstein. Not every kid with aberrant behavior is a genius but every genius is atypical. As we pursue our child's fixations, some of us will find exceptional talent.

The questions below will help you pinpoint your child's special interest or affinity. They don't have to be an expert at it; it just has to hold their attention more than other things. It might be Popsicle sticks, bugs, the color purple, or wheels. Once you know what holds their attention, I believe you can use it to teach them almost anything: vocabulary, writing, math, geography, conversation skills, even grammar. You cannot teach anything if you don't have your child's attention. So use the special interest to gain and keep that.

*What do you notice gives your child joy?*

*Is there something your child seems to do better than their peers?*

*What could your child rise early or stay up all night doing without you?*

# 5

## *Keep the Tempo*

## Teach to the Strength

## Keep the Tempo

*Tempo means time. It sets the mood of a piece of music. Historically, one purpose of music was to accompany people who were dancing. The movement of the dancers' feet and body positions set the tempo of the music, and the musicians followed the dancers. Although the metronome was the perfect invention for control freaks, most composers were happy to use the growing vocabulary of Italian terms like* largo, lento, adagio, vivace, *and* prestissimo *to describe the pace of a song.*

*A great teacher is the one who can teach challenged learners not just the typical ones. One of the keys is their ability to step in time with the student, find a tempo that is mutually beneficial, and teach to the child's strengths. That is when a love of learning results.*

# 5

## Teach to the Strength

*I believe that all genial classrooms share at least five characteristics that guide their instruction regardless of content or grade level. These characteristics are (1) freedom to choose, (2) open-ended exploration, (3) freedom from judgment, (4) honoring every student's experience, and (5) belief in every student's genius.*

—THOMAS ARMSTRONG, PHD

Once you know your child's special interest, teach the heck out of it. When you teach from this position of their preference, your child will pay attention, be motivated, and learn more, faster than if you hammer away at their weaknesses or subject matter that seems irrelevant to them. If they're anything like Reid, their weaknesses outnumber their strengths, thereby threatening to hog your attention. Resist this temptation to drill and kill. Or your child will also resist. Temple Grandin, the renowned autism activist and professor of animal science, agrees, "There needs to be a lot more emphasis on what a child can do instead of what he cannot do."

A special education preschool teacher noticed Reid's affinity for music and how dramatically his attention span increased when they used music. One afternoon, she asked me, "Have you ever considered music therapy?" At that time, I hadn't heard of it, but took her referral and called Barbara Reuer of MusicWorx.[6] Barbara graduates a new crop of music therapy interns in San Diego every semester. Reid has had a music therapist for the fifteen years since I called Barbara. The first one, Michelle Lazar, who later founded Coast Music Therapy, was a key member of Reid's home-program team when he was five. She participated in weekly team meetings to coordinate efforts with a behavioral therapist, speech therapist, occupational therapist, and various tutors. Once a week, she facilitated playgroups with kids from our neighborhood to help Reid practice greetings, social skills, and turn taking. His sixth birthday party was a music-therapy circle time she led with interactive activities and movement songs he loved. Just add friends (and scarves and cake).

The parents of the typical children who were invited were grateful for the opportunity and extra education their kids received by virtue of participating. They were practicing creativity, encouragement, inclusion, patience, and new modes of communication. Michelle modeled and supported ways that they could be friends and effective communicators at school with all their peers. Early, constructive exposure to children who learn and behave differently can spark special interests and gifts—like teaching, compassion, persistence, and justice—in the typical children who interact with our children. Picturing their little faces, I realize some of the preschoolers at that birthday party, and in those Integrated

---

6 MusicWorx Inc. is a provider of music therapy services and an American Music Therapy Association–approved clinical training site for degreed music therapists working toward national board certification founded in 1987.

Playgroups,[7] went on to write assignments in high school about knowing Reid and what they learned from interacting with him.

Michelle wrote songs for all Reid's IEP goals: sensory integration, self-regulation, addition, subtraction, and oral motor. You name it; we had a song for it. I still wonder if it was sacrilege when she substituted the lyrics of several of the *My First Hymnal* hits Reid preferred to target goals like refusing gluten. "No pretzels. No bagels. No crackers. No cookies. No, no, no, no, no, no, no gluten! Makes me feel sick." We cross-trained the entire team so all his tutors could support him with music, even the ones working on potty training. There's a song for that!

Music therapy worked. And Reid was a poster child for its effectiveness. He could communicate and engage when music was involved. In a nonmusic setting he was, and still is, uncomfortable, agitated, and disengaged. Turn the music on and you have his total attention. It was the only therapy he didn't avoid. Therapy, by definition, works on something that is hard for you, whether that is rehabilitating a shoulder or saying the "th" sound. For a kid on the spectrum with a forty hour a week intervention program, everything is hard. Music, however, is intrinsically pleasurable, transforming the difficult tasks into play. Kathleen Howland, a professor at Berklee College of Music, says of her beloved colleagues, "Music therapists come, not to entertain but primarily to create neural changes that result in functional outcomes to address stress, pain, fear, language, speech, cognition, movement, or lasting differences. They do all this embedded in a clinical relationship of empathy, compassion, and service."

---

7 Integrated Play Groups® is a research-validated model originated by Pamela Wolfberg, PhD, to promote socialization, communication, play, and imagination in children with autism, while building relationships with typical peers and siblings through mutually engaging experiences in natural settings.

In many ways, I felt like music therapy gave Reid back his childhood. It was fun and compensated him for the grueling effort he was expending to learn the simplest of tasks that seemed to come by osmosis to other kids. Howland puts it this way, "Music is non-invasive, inviting, comforting, motivational, fun, and gives meaning. It has the ability to maximize and sustain our effort, whether in gym class or for those bygone sailors who created sea shanties to strengthen their cooperative efforts pulling in rigging for hours on end." Sadly, in 1998 music therapy was considered icing on the cake or an unnecessary luxury, like arts programs are in so many schools. For Reid though, it was clearly the anchor that grounded him.

To be honest, I wanted some of my own music therapy. It was therapeutic enough to overhear my children so completely engaged and joyful in the family room, but eventually I did sign up for a session after theirs. I needed a refresher course in piano to be able to help them practice. More than once, I was aware that the therapist was serving me as much as teaching me the chords. She selected jazz pieces that required me to loosen up, made me improvise, and listened a lot to my ramblings before we even opened the assignment book. If I was ranting or in knots, she would transition in a thinly veiled counselor voice. "Why don't we start with this today?" Her back pockets were loaded with tools for using music to achieve nonmusic goals, even for emotionally weary caregivers.

There was a time I said, "Everything Reid knows he learned through music: potty training, skip counting, the alphabet, grammar, Bible verses, planets." We tapped homeschooling catalogs for resources using music to teach. *Sing, Spell, Read and Write* was the reading curriculum of choice, and we literally wore out cassettes like Barbara Milne's *Sounds Like Fun*. Reid and Allie both learned the tenets of our faith from Judy Rogers's *Go to the Ant* CD and memorized Bible verses with Steve Green's Hide 'em in Your Heart series. Two of our initial young music therapists—Michelle and Angela Neve—went on to publish excellent resources comprised of songs they used with Reid, including: "No Gluten," "Ways to Say Hello," "Talking Loudly and Softly," "Listening to What My Body Says," and "The Coin Song." Reid and I highly recommend *Tuned into Learning* and *In Harmony* as easy-to-use tools for home or classrooms.

This Teach-to-the-Strength principle refers to both "what" you teach and "how" you teach it. Once you have identified the affinity or passion, teach to that subject matter or modality in every way possible. It is also hugely helpful to know your child's strengths, and be able to articulate them to others. One of the best tools for doing this is the *StrengthsFinder* online assessment. After a twenty-minute web-based test, it determines a person's top five strengths. We have done this for each member of our family, and it has become foundational to how we interact, learn, and appreciate one another. Very likely there will be a relationship between your child's special interest and his strengths. Reid loves music, and his strengths profile is that of a performer. Jim has a special interest in technology and the strengths of an executive. It is not a direct correlation, but you will start to see the pieces fit together.

One can always remediate the weakness, but new learning will be most effectively done through the pathway of the strength. Tom Rath, *New York Times* bestselling author of *StrengthsFinder 2.0,* is concerned about the "way our fixation on deficits affects young people in the home and classroom. In every culture we have studied, the overwhelming majority of parents think that a student's *lowest* grades deserve the *most* attention. Parents and teachers reward excellence with apathy instead of investing more time in the areas where a child has the most potential for greatness.

Rather than taking the path of most resistance…the key to human development is building on who you *already* are." I think the *StrengthsFinder* online assessment is the best investment you can make for less than twenty dollars. The results it yields are a valuable counterpoint to the deficit-based IEPs that dictate our students' programs. It is available in a *StrengthsFinder Jr.* version that can be adapted to most people on the spectrum, even if completed by a surrogate. Add it as a page to your IEP.

While we're on the topic of IEP meetings, don't ever go to one alone. They are sensible in theory; all the members of your child's team gather to review annual goals, levels of functioning, services, and placement. In practice, however, they seldom satisfy. As wonderful as the individuals who sit around the table and interact with our kids are, they are part of a system that is designed to do the least amount possible to serve kids who don't fit the mold. I used to take muffins and aim to be friends with every participant on the team. Our meetings were three hours at a minimum and often tabled to resume another day for another three hours.

You can imagine how this flew with my executive husband. He is so efficient and decisive he only reads the first line of e-mails. In an IEP meeting, Jim would look at his watch, then at me across the table with that face that said, "I have *got* to leave." His eyes would expand, and if I didn't know him better, I would have thought his bladder was full from a sixty-four-ounce Slurpee they'd forced him to drink. Trying to be polite, he would attempt to steamroll the meeting to some conclusion. "How much longer do you think this will take?" "What's our goal here?" The process was so inefficient and expensive to his business frame of mind; it was agonizing to sit through.

When we wanted a particular placement one year, I enlisted the help of an advocate who was less expensive than a full-fledged attorney. Can I tell you? The difference was night and day. She placed phone calls beforehand to the decision makers, preempted all counterpoints and objections, orchestrated the whole process, and smoked heavily. The first meeting she attended with us was the first one that was under an hour. I looked at her and said, "I am never going to an IEP without you." A vivid spiritual parallel presented itself. I sure don't want to be standing before God on judgment day without Christ as my advocate. (1 John 2) It will make all the difference to have Him present who is the law and has paid the price for my sins. For now, it makes all the difference to have someone present that knows the law and calls the administrators to task. Then, you can actually stay friends with the ones who spend all day with your child. Having an advocate also freed Jim up to stay at his office and work, where he's most effective. Now he only comes if I need "moron support," as he calls it.

—⸙—

A sense of humor is one of the most underestimated self-care skills and indicators of healthy acceptance. I recall the shift in time from when we were mad at the world to when we were able to laugh. Laughing, like music, is good medicine that served as a release valve on the pressure cooker of demands that came with a high-maintenance child. Being a spontaneous extrovert, Jim is more playful than me, and way funnier. He mixes up words on purpose, asking if I was just being "fastidious" when he means "facetious" and still throws random items—like fuzzy slippers— in my grocery cart just for a reaction. When he picks Allie up at the airport, he has been known to stand in a line of livery drivers with a handmade placard lettered with her nickname. I never knew how advantageous it would be to marry the class clown.

When Reid does something odd in public, like adjust the Brute lids on the industrial garbage cans at a trailhead, chuckling affectionately with Jim beats the alienation and challenge that could come from taking everything too seriously. It reminds me that we are in this together and frees me up to enjoy the adventure of life. When Allie is home from college, there are even more winks, inside jokes, and family camaraderie. We find ourselves in a fair share of awkward situations with Reid, whether reshelving VHS tapes in a thrift store or preempting his gag reflex at the sight of ketchup in restaurants. It helps to have jovial company. Stephen Colbert explains it well. "We can't laugh and be afraid at the same time. That's the purpose of humor. We laugh when we're afraid because our body is trying to get rid of the fear inside us. The only way to approach something that's really hard has got to be with joy; if you don't it's just a machine that will grind you up. Doing something joyfully doesn't make it any easier. It only makes it better and communal. When you work in fear or distress, you often feel alone."

Humor releases Reid from a stuck place, too. I used to include it on my Top 5 List of helpful hints for babysitters. (1. Don't take it personally. 2. Make it visual. 3. Use humor. 4. Avoid power struggles. 5. Give advance notice and stay ten steps ahead of Reid.) One day when he was in fourth grade, my mom was babysitting. Reid could not, would not, did not, get dressed for school. In an attempt to drop him off on time, she managed to get him physically in the car in his pajamas, with a change of clothes in hand. His teacher greeted them at the curb and used humor to budge him. "Reid, did you think it was pajama day? You can't go in like that." Laughter loosens our need to dig in our heels.

Thomas Armstrong, PhD and educational consultant, wrote a fabulous book titled *Neurodiversity*, which looks at the upside of discovering the unique gifts within labels like autism, ADHD, and dyslexia. He tells how he used to comb through a student's cumulative file before an IEP and mark all the positive statements with a highlighter. He then typed these highlighted bits into a new document and distributed it to begin the meeting. It transformed the attitudes of the team around the table and the dialogue that ensued. "I'd notice that many adults at the meeting would express surprise at the number of positive things said about a student who was so troubled and/or troubling to others." He continues, "The process of investigating the positive dimensions of people with negative labels can make a world of difference in helping them achieve success in life." Beginning with these positives, strengths, talents, abilities, and special interests can drive better decisions and solutions.

Teaching to the Strength is so effective and intuitive; some students figure it out themselves. Owen Suskind taught himself to read by carefully watching the movie credits scroll at the end of Disney films. Pairing new skills or content with music still enables us to tackle new subjects with Reid and expand his preference for what is familiar. He was insistent throughout his schooling, often communicating through his behavior, that teachers teach to his strength; music was his obvious channel for learning. If your child is not doing that, don't wait for the system. You may have to be the one to advocate for teaching in new ways or supplement at home.

I learned the hard way that more is not necessarily better when it comes to therapies. I am grateful we had the resources to try almost everything available, short of swimming with dolphins. Jim used to chide me, "What is the flavor of the month, this month?"

He couldn't keep up with all the training trips to learn Floortime[8] in Washington, DC, Maverick Mind in Ohio, psychomotor patterning, and Brain Highways, let alone how to give the B12 shots or collect samples for the biomedical interventions. Did they all help? No. And some of them hurt. Would I do it all over again? Maybe, but not all of them. Be a wise consumer and trust that if a particular program is really the key for your child, then it will be God's provision to make it affordable for you. I think very often we were stepping outside of trusting Him when we grabbed at expensive straws that *might* help.

In addition to trying everything, manically following protocols, and plastering the house with picture cards and visuals, I tended to hide behind books in the early years. I guess I thought if I could know it all, then maybe I could control it all. There again, I neglected the supreme omniscience of the One who created my son. He knew which authors, books, professionals, and therapies would be worth our time, money, and energy. I should've consulted Him first and more often. A friend of mine made a critical decision when she decided to quit fighting and start praying. I learned how to pray in many new ways: declaring scripture over my kids, rebuking obstacles, and asking for specific strategy as if life were a battle and God was the commander. There is more happening than we can see.

We had a most unlikely turn of events choosing a home-program supervisor when Reid was five years old. The school district had an agency they always used. While the agency was reputable, I had a gut instinct that we should work with a younger woman who was new in town. Amazingly, we had met her in northern California

---

8 Floortime is a strategy of the DIR model developed by Stanley Greenspan. Focusing on the building blocks of healthy development, this approach emphasizes the creation of emotionally meaningful learning exchanges that encourage developmental abilities.

when we lived there. She confided that she would be moving back to San Diego within months of us. I thought that had to be a sign, among other things, that she was the one for us. I expressed my preference, and we interviewed both providers, but the district was set on keeping their existing contract. Feeling rather desperate at that point to turn my vulnerable pre-K boy over to hours on end of therapy with strangers, I was compelled to pray for God's will. Most of the night, I asked God to take care of it. Would you believe the next morning the contracted agency took themselves out of the running. They told the district, "We sense the mother would prefer to work with the new provider." Invite God to your IEP meetings; He loves to show off in impossible situations.

Giving us children may be God's grand plan to get us on our knees, talking to Him on a daily basis, just like when we put Reid's toys up high on a chair-rail shelf in his room so he'd have a reason to talk to us. He got what he wanted (the toys) and so did we (the engagement). Something about our children makes us so protective, defensive of criticism, and desperate for solutions. It must be exactly how God feels about each of us. He is willing to do whatever it takes to engage with us. The difference is He knows what it will take and we don't. Therein lies the reason again, to pray and ask Him and keep on asking.

Preparing for IEP meetings, selecting therapists, and investigating schools can feel like bushwhacking through a jungle of information overload. One has to be discerning amid the consumerism that is the special needs world right now. Every specialist is selling only what they know, as if it were the turnkey, ultimate truth and solution for your child. The problem is, how can they be so sure?

As much as I disdain the autism puzzle-piece icon, raising our kids is like working a puzzle without the image on the box top. As Jim says, "All bets are off." It seems to require the myopic view of an intentional and engrossed parent to crack the code. Advising another dad whose son was just diagnosed, Jim recently shared this: "Very few doctors are going to create a plan for you. Insanely creative and driven moms are going to do that. You'll need to navigate this stage and get close to some mavens who won't have 'doctor' in front of their names. Not to paint too broadly: some docs are awesome. I've just seen moms who are better."

Teach to your child's strength and help their teachers do the same by providing notes and lots of dialogue back and forth from school. The more relevant lessons and activities are, the more your child will want to learn and enjoy learning. They may not be able to do everything, so we need to maximize what they can and will do. That's where their special interest becomes a tool to leverage the basics like spelling and vocabulary, math, writing, and language and make them come alive for your child. The customization takes time, but not nearly as much as we might waste with an uninterested student.

*What are your child's strengths (Use your own words or the StrengthsFinder terms like Relator, Woo, Positivity, Discipline, Command, Learner, and Belief)?*

*How are you already teaching to that strength?*

*What are your strengths? Do you know what strengths your spouse, teachers, grandparents, neighbors, and siblings bring to the table?*

# 6

## *Make Loud Mistakes*

## Experiment to Find a Niche

## Make Loud Mistakes

*Music students tire of hearing this adage. Naturally, we all prefer to hide the embarrassment of our mistakes. Yet, becoming a musician who plays with gusto and confidence may require a willingness to risk an occasional loud mistake. The result is more likely to create a compelling and worthy performance or recording. It is better to give all you've got with passion and feeling than be paralyzed by perfectionism or fear.*

*Like loosening up your writing before worrying about spelling or punctuation, making loud mistakes enables freedom of expression and our best creativity. Finding a niche in life can sometimes be a matter of trial and error. The louder the errors, the quicker we can move on to striking the right chord.*

# 6

## Experiment to Find a Niche

*I like the fact that in ancient Chinese art the great painters always included a deliberate flaw in their work: human creation is never perfect.*

—Madeleine L'Engle

Teaching to your child's strength gets easier as you incorporate it into daily life. You will start thinking like them and seeing teachable moments that are within their wheelhouse. Another principle we employed was to experiment to find a niche. Although we knew Reid loved music early on, we didn't stumble upon his niche of performing until later. Armstrong can't overstate the importance of this: "Positive niche construction directly modifies the brain, which in turn enhances its ability to adapt to the environment. Thus, positive niche construction in the earliest years of life should be the number-one priority for parents."

Reid played soccer for one season, but the team dynamics made no sense to him. He tried swim team and is a beautiful swimmer, but the acoustics are often problematic at pools. We skied as a family until the year of the outburst. Let's just say, it is hard to manage a meltdown in ski boots in a chairlift line. I created a Sign Camp when Reid was about seven years old and could write his name—a hard-won skill that had frustrated several occupational therapists. He liked to read street signs at the time, so it seemed signage might hold his attention and enable some progress on his fine-motor goals. We could "write" with brushes, rollers, chalk, markers, and crayons. With Allie and a neighbor boy, we read *The Legend of Slappy Hooper*, a tall tale about the biggest, "bestest," and fastest sign painter around, visited a local sign painter, and posted handmade signs up and down our street. Reid took an art class, but his fine-motor skills were a frustration, and for some reason, he would systematically scribble over each masterpiece at the end of class. Experimenting and trying new things eventually opened doors to a niche perfectly suited to Reid. Taking these exploratory risks was part and parcel of discovering his niche.

Music therapists tend to be empathetic, inclusive, relational, and adept at not just encouraging, but actually developing skills in others. We have gotten to know a dozen of them over the years, none as well as Angela Neve, cofounder of The Music Therapy Center of California, who we have seen weekly for nearly thirteen years. I fondly remember the Fridays when she made music with every member of the family, in turn. After her session with Reid, she started Allie on the flute. She saw me for piano refresher lessons, and then Jim dusted off the guitar that stood in the corner of his closet. One year, Angela arranged a touching and hilarious version of the "Mexican Hat Dance" that we, the "Flying Moriachis," played at her annual recital. I kid you not. If Angela would have moved in, we would have built an addition.

When Reid was nine, she invited him to perform with her at an NBC Health Fair where she was marketing her newly formed business among the wellness services. The event was in downtown San Diego, about thirty minutes from our home. Getting there on time with a clean shirt and shoes was easier said than done. It meant navigating the obstacles and stimuli of an unfamiliar urban environment. I was most aware of a four-story Tower Records we would have to circumnavigate in order to get from our car on Level K4 in the parking garage to the event in the NBC Plaza. That black hole created stress and threatened to sabotage the entire experience.

I prepped Reid the whole drive down. "When we get there, we are going to hold hands, cross the busy streets, and stay together. We can go to Tower Records *after* the show if you do a good job, but not before. There will be lots of people so we have to stick together and find Angela. That's the first thing." I quizzed him for comprehension. "When will we go to Tower?"

"After I sing." He got it.

"Right." With minutes to spare before the call time, I gripped both Allie and Reid by the hand beside the car in a moment of resolve.

Sensing the importance and tension, Reid looked up at me and said, "Mom, just get me to the stage."

That was his first gig, and many more would follow. A sort of Clark Kent syndrome took over once he was on the stage. He was appropriate, self-aware, strangely "able," undeniably in his element. He remembered all the lyrics and surprised his teacher in the audience with a shout-out. Afterward, he was pumped with adrenaline-fueled language and neurological connectedness that made us want to bottle and sell the whole experience. It was amazing. He was fluent, coherent, even chatty as we drove home. Like a surfer coming out of the water after an epic session, he was calm, cool, and connected.

Angela had taken his special interest to the next level. As an objective third party who lived outside the trenches, she was uniquely able to conceptualize and implement this new launch pad for his special interest and strength, while I dealt with the more mundane annoyances like getting around video stores. Operating outside those obstacles, her vision for his potential was clearer. She had identified his innate performer and was channeling his attention-seeking behaviors into something positive. The practice and rehearsal components of music performance suited his brain and helped him succeed. Music therapy for Reid had morphed from addressing his IEP goals to becoming adapted music lessons and now, to engaging in the community and working on life skills.

Most people, myself included, dread being on stage. I function well in typical social settings, but put me in the limelight and I freeze in panic. Reid was the opposite, awkward in daily life, unable to understand money concepts, conversation, and typical social interaction. Put him on stage though, and he knew exactly what to do. In fact, he sought the stage. Anywhere there was a stage or a microphone, he gravitated toward it, whether to help announce raffle ticket winners or sing backup with a street performer. We were opposite and complementary, like blue and orange. Not as much as he and Allie, but a close second. (When we get pizza, he eats the cheese and she eats the crust.) We were also a good team; I could get him to the stage, then he could have the spotlight. The stage was his niche.

Discovering a niche for our children requires taking some risks. When we brace ourselves with courage and let them try something new, we send an empowering message through our behavior. I can think of friends who have had to be brave and watch while their child helped brand calves at a dude ranch, join the cheerleading squad at a high school football game, travel with a girls' volleyball team to away games, stand on a street corner twirling an advertising sign, and leave on a bus for overnight camp. Each of those experiences took them to a new level, even if it wasn't completely successful. One friend of mine applied the 70/30 rule to everything her son did. Since no program, therapy, or person is perfect, she considered it successful, or good enough, if it was 70 percent beneficial. Some ideas may fail, even by the 70/30 rule, and that's fine. Even if our kids don't succeed, they still grow. We can celebrate the attempt of something new and make their world a safe place to fail.

One flop of mine that comes to mind was a Dot-to-Dot birthday party we had the year Reid was consumed with them. Guests were given a number nametag when they arrived, and I tried to maneuver live action dot-to-dot formations from the top of our swing-set play structure. Jim was to take string and connect them. Like I said, some experiments don't work. The neighbor dad who accompanied his son to this unusual party was gracious to not mention it ever again. We had other more successful social opportunities like Movie Night in our backyard and an annual Christmas Caroling party. Anything to engage Reid was our definition of success for many years.

Is there something new your child could try? Don't be afraid to make a loud mistake. Go ahead and experiment. It may require a favor of someone, extra staff, or modifications, but if you have reason to believe it suits your child and might help them pursue their special interest, take the risk to find out whether it might become their niche. If it goes exceedingly well, it could change the course of your child's life.

*What are your three proudest moments with your child?*

*Has a nonfamily member ever suggested something far-fetched that your child might actually do?*

*Has your child expressed any lofty goals?*

# 7

## *Adjust Dynamics*

Adapt As Age Appropriate

## *Adjust Dynamics*

*Dynamics in music communicate volume and intensity.* Piano, forte, *and other markings help musicians interpret the expressive quality of the music. Dynamics give the music meaning.* "When the Saints Go Marching In" *is a song traditionally associated with the city of New Orleans. It is usually performed at a fast (*allegro*) tempo, with loud (*forte*) dynamics, and in a happy, major key like a celebration. If a composer or performer wants to send a different message, they might change the dynamic to play the song slowly (*lento*), quietly (*piano*), and in a sad, minor key, making the song sound mournful as if the whole city or nation is grieving after the destruction of Hurricane Katrina.*

*Adapting a child's special interest to their age is like adjusting the dynamics on a piece of music. Using the child's preferred special interest is like a familiar piece of music that ensures their engagement. Within a comfortable context, the child is confident and willing to move to the next level or change the dynamics of the tune, as it were. Pairing something familiar with a new variation or skill is an effective way to challenge the child without undue resistance or distress.*

# 7

## Adapt As Age Appropriate

*All I really need to know...I learned in kindergarten.*

—ROBERT FULGHUM, *NEW YORK TIMES*
BESTSELLING AUTHOR

Almost every special interest can grow with your child, as they mature into a teenager and young adult. As teachers and parents, we may need to drive the adaptation, but it is possible. Approaching a passion from another angle will keep it relevant and age-appropriate to the outside world as well as to your developing child. For example, I imagine trains were an obsession of Walt Disney's long after his mother packed away the bulky wooden track pieces. The special interest grew with him, inspiring his very grown-up enterprise of Disneyland. Playmobil Toys can be turned into stop-action figures for the budding videographer, as another example. A teen still obsessed with baby books can research the authors and illustrators or read them to preschoolers.

Music, being the universal language, develops easily with the learner. Take it from Paul Simon, "music is forever; music should grow and mature with you, following you right on up until you die."

When Reid was thirteen, Angela wisely observed, "Every teenager wants to be in a band. Why can't these guys with autism be in one, too?" She grouped four young men on the spectrum together to form a band. They named themselves the Kingsmen. Imagine for a minute, a cluster of adolescent boys with peach fuzz and pimples in a practice room, each with a different instrument—and their own idiosyncrasies—deciding what song to play. This was either a horrible idea or a brilliant one; there was no space for anything in between. The Kingsmen rehearsed once a week; the guitarist changed a couple times, and they all became close friends due to proximity as well as their shared passion for music. They remain so today and the band plays on.

As you can imagine, being in a band requires social skills, group learning, self-advocacy, taking turns, discipline to practice, and self-expression. They learned all these things and continued to practice them by doing them in a strengths-based setting through their special interest of music. And it was age appropriate, to boot.

The Kingsmen averaged a gig a month for five years, including the annual Autism Walk, multiple coffeehouses and fund-raising soirees. Taking them out of the music therapy clinic to set up gear, introduce their own songs, and play in public settings required boldness, ingenuity, and optimism, all of which Angela had, even if we did not. She was dealing with four autistic adolescents, four highly engaged mothers, four executive fathers, and two siblings thrown in for good measure when they could play in on bass or flute.

Over time, we came to trust Angela's willingness to experiment and iterate a new threshold for the boys' ability. We would never forget their first gig, though: a holiday open house at a Borders bookstore. Without any precedent, it was nerve-racking, mostly for the parents. We were anxious about how the audience would react. How would they receive or respond to our awkward, vulnerable, quirky at best, boys? We feared rejection, humiliation, and ridicule. As soon as the last "...jingle all the way" chorus concluded, three of the four moms headed out the store straightaway, heads bowed, looking for their keys. Jim was the only dad present. We hung around (partly because Reid was scoping out the video displays) and were pleasantly surprised to hear from several patrons who had seen the show. The unprepared audience of shoppers had been mesmerized. They formed their own conclusions about our boys; it was obvious how much effort they invested in the performance as well as how much fun they were having. Those who stopped to watch were thankful and genuinely touched by hearing these unique voices.

With time and practice, we moms relaxed and learned not to apologize for our sons. Though imperfect, their voices were important. The dads eventually hovered proudly with cameras, giving future audiences permission to laugh and be imperfect themselves. We learned to trust the public, and a sort of audience therapy unfolded inevitably in each new venue. The boys delivered their own brand of feel-good, can-do encouragement. Reid never failed to "get the crowd going" throwing his hands in the air modeling an overhead clap for them to join or enticing them to "sing along if you know the words!"

For the passerby as well as some die-hard Kingsmen fans, a public appearance provided a way for them to encourage and participate in the life of the underdog. Very often, people want to help a family with special needs but don't quite know how to, especially as their new normal, challenging life sets in and their child gets older. These concerts gave our friends and neighbors an opportunity to observe and interact with Reid that they struggled to find on Sunday morning after church or even if they dropped by our house. It brought the boys out of the margins and into the spotlight. Scaffolding our children's special interests provides a platform where their abilities can be celebrated and they can interact positively with people, as opposed to being perceived as needy, aimless, intimidating, or (God forbid) worthless.

Not that they weren't still needy. It took an entourage to schlep the gear and persuade the boys to help. Each of them had caveats and complaints behind the scenes. One nearly fell asleep drumming at a gig that was after his strict, self-imposed bedtime. Another verbally objected to sharing a microphone, being in direct sun, and being touched.

"I can't share a microphone. May I please have my own?"

Reid would scoot the mic over to let him have it, but bump him in the process.

"Reid, you touched me. What do you say?"

"Uh," was all we heard, but the crowd could fill in the cartoon bubble over his head. Reid's was a physical comedy where the way he turned his head would crack you up.

The two had comedic timing that rivaled Jack Klugman and Tony Randall in the old *Odd Couple* sitcom. Something about Reid's ginger cowlicks and jaunty air made him look crumpled even in a new polo shirt. By the time we reached the gig it would inevitably be smeared with sunscreen, pollen, or refried beans. He could easily outdo the wear tests that Sears, Roebuck and Co. designed for Toughskins; now that distressed jeans are in vogue, he's a hipster.

His buddy was a paragon of perfection, the straight man. Tucked in and belted, his wardrobe looked so crisp you could return it without a receipt when he outgrew each item. He watched like a sheriff for violations of every code and safety precaution known to man. If an amplifier cord lay across the stage he would warn others.

"Be careful. Don't trip on that cord."

"This cord?" Reid seemed like he might demonstrate how that would look with a roll into a somersault at the end, perhaps.

They were the making of great comedy. It was a hoot. Their unrehearsed antics sharing a mic or just portraying opposites, became a favorite part of the shtick.

Each bandmate had a characteristic way to "get in the zone" backstage before a performance. One paced; another checked that the cords and equipment were in order. Reid consistently lay flat on his back on the floor to get acclimated. It didn't matter whether it was the sawdust and dirt floor of the San Diego Fairgrounds or the green room of the Belly Up Tavern. This was his way of assimilating with the venue (and checking out their ceiling). I suppose all rock stars have a ritual of some sort on tour.

Before the Kingsmen opened for Willie Nelson's son's band, I patted the bandmate who didn't like to be touched on the shoulder with a hearty, "Good luck out there!" He more than bristled. Time nearly stopped as I gasped. "*Ooooooo*, I totally forgot. I am so sorry...," I pantomimed behind the stage curtain, fearing I had botched their entrance, if not the whole evening. Amazingly, the audience never knew of my cardinal sin. The boys had a sense of responsibility to the crowd and always, in all ways, pulled it together. The show must go on was their modus operandi.

Reid liked to see the venues in advance so he would know what to expect, so we often drove by them the week before. Still, his stock response to an invitation to a new place is, "I'll consider it."

Waiting for the other shoe to drop had become a lifestyle at least for us, so I held my breath a little before every performance back then. The shoe, let's call it, did drop as I exited the off-ramp for a gig at a large hotel. From the back of our Volkswagen Eurovan, the hotel-on-wheels, as we called it, Reid announced, "Mom, I have a poop alert."

*What? Now? Oh no,* I thought. "OK, don't worry, we'll find a place to go," I promised.

This was harder than it might sound. Reid had an assortment of requirements for public bathrooms. They must not have automatic flushers. They must offer total privacy. There must be no wait time and no one waiting. He was too old to go in the women's room with me. Without Jim to run interference in a men's room, it was even trickier. He has as many conditions on public restrooms as I did for being able to read fine print. My failing eyes work well, but only when I open them extra wide, have full sunlight, and tilt the book at just the right angle. When the conditions were right, neither of us needed correction or assistance. I think going to the bathroom made him more anxious than performing, but couple the two and his nerves were fraying. I thought I might wet *my* pants.

"It's all better. I don't have to go anymore, Mom."

"Um, what do you mean?"

I smelled the answer. *I better have a change of clothes in here somewhere.* Rather than risk embarrassment at the venue, I pulled into a Denny's parking lot, and we solved the problem. As I said, *whatever* challenges we had before or after, he always pulled it together and never failed to entertain.

The Kingsmen were telling their story through song. Independent from their musicianship (which was improving), music—and specifically performance—was giving them a way to engage with the world. Their unique life experience imparted new meaning to the songs they covered. In a strangely similar way, the movie *Young at Heart* documents a choir of senior citizens who tour the world, singing popular rock covers. The maturity and circumstances of these octogenarians lends a new dimension to the song lyrics, enabling them to communicate volumes about their experience. In the poignant closing scene of the movie, an aging man delivers Coldplay's hit, "Fix You," in tribute to his duet partner who died just before the group's European tour date. The lyrics are punctuated by the pulsing hiss of his oxygen machine like an eerie metronome.

*When you try your best, but you don't succeed*
*When you get what you want, but not what you need*
*When you feel so tired, but you can't sleep*
*Stuck in reverse*

*And the tears come streaming down your face*
*When you lose something you can't replace*
*When you love someone, but it goes to waste*
*Could it be worse?*

*Lights will guide you home*
*And ignite your bones*
*And I will try to fix you*

One December, the Kingsmen were invited to play all three Sunday services at our church. It would be a challenge to occupy the boys backstage for the forty-five minutes they were not singing, let alone between services, but we agreed. It was imperfect and impressive. Reid sat crisscross applesauce at the grand piano and plunked out the hand position of his opening chord as the pastor introduced them. Their voices were undeniably powerful that advent as they sang with growing confidence the lyrics from The Killers' song, "All These Things that I've Done."

*Help me out*
*Yeah, you know you got to help me out*
*Yeah, oh don't you put me on the backburner*
*You know you got to help me out*

*And when there's nowhere else to run*
*Is there room for one more son*
*These changes ain't changing me*
*The cold-hearted boy I used to be*

*Yeah, you know you got to help me out*
*Yeah, oh don't you put me on the backburner*
*You know you got to help me out*
*You're gonna bring yourself down*

*I got soul, but I'm not a soldier*
*I got soul, but I'm not a soldier*
*I got soul, but I'm not a soldier*

Without trying or realizing it, they drove home the message that unexpected visitors were welcome at the manger that first Christmas. They had credibility to say what no one else could have from the narthex. The congregation responded by clapping along to the chorus and bursting to their feet at the end.

Another time, Reid sang solo at a committee kickoff event for the local Walk Now for Autism event. We were seated at a front banquet table, waiting for his turn in the program. It came after a lengthy and inopportune presentation by a leading researcher on burgeoning strides in stem cell research. She was making an awkward plea for brain tissue donation from children who may not live to their full expectancy.

Jim, Allie, and I watched with widening eyes, wondering a.) How was Reid internalizing this message? and b.) Was the irony obvious to everyone else as Reid stepped forward to sing "The Scientist" by Coldplay?

> *Tell me your secrets*
> *And ask me your questions*
> *Oh let's go back to the start*
> *Running in circles; coming up tails*
> *Heads on a science apart*
>
> *Nobody said it was easy*
> *It's such a shame for us to part*
> *Nobody said it was easy*
> *No one ever said it would be this hard*
> *Oh take me back to the start*
>
> *I was just guessing at numbers and figures*
> *Pulling your puzzles apart*
> *Questions of science; science and progress*
> *Do not speak as loud as my heart*

There he was, front and center, with his anomalous brain, communicating more through his inability than the scientists could articulate in reams of journals. Even Angela couldn't have planned that, although her intuition for choosing repertoire was uncannily good.

Pulling at heartstrings seems apropos at fund-raisers. The Kingsmen did that without trying. Another emotional night was the first-ever San Diego Young Life Capernaum Soiree. We had rented a funky urban rooftop to reenact the namesake story from the Gospel of Luke. Some exceptional friends go to great lengths to get their friend with special needs to the feet of Jesus in the town of Capernaum. They lower him through the thatch roof on a pallet. To make matters even more accurate to biblical times, the power went out that night in the entire county. There we were with two of the four Kingsmen and a small fraction of the expected guests. The stalwart supporters who made it downtown despite the blackout and traffic that ensued, had to climb twelve flights of stairs, since the elevator was also out.

We greatly abbreviated the program and instead of the set list they had rehearsed, Conor and Reid picked one song and gave it their best shot. Unplugged, with Angela on acoustic guitar, they proclaimed the words of an already convicting song by Switchfoot, "This is Your Life."

*This is your life, are you who you want to be?*
*This is your life, are you who you want to be?*
*This is your life, is it everything you dreamed that it would be?*
*When the world was younger and you had everything to lose*

*Don't close your eyes*
*Don't close your eyes*
*Don't close your eyes*

In the pitch dark, over the increasing din of sirens and emergency vehicles, on the roof above the fray, they asked the gathered leaders, caterers, and precious few potential donors the profound question of the night. It was not a typical fund-raiser; not a typical cause, not a typical venue, not a typical act. That's just it, I guess. It wasn't an act; it was real. These boys invited others to give all they had. Their perfectly imperfect voices moved the intimate crowd like pins dropping in harmony. I think people heard more in the absence of a keyboard, amp, and lights. The reenactment continued exactly as Luke 5:26 records it in The Message, "The people rubbed their eyes, incredulous—and then also gave glory to God. Awestruck, they said, 'We've never seen anything like that!'"

Whatever your child's special interest, it can be adapted and made relevant as your student becomes a teenager and adult. These teenage boys were performing Top 40 popular songs in public settings, which was socially appropriate for their stage in life, even if their musical ability was more in line with what you might expect at an elementary school music recital. Music could grow with them, as could their awareness of the world and the world's awareness of them.

♭

One of Reid's bus drivers reminded me of this Adapt-As-Age-Appropriate principle. As he boarded the bus for home from middle school, she overheard a teacher prohibit him from talking about *Barney* because it was too babyish. She told me, "I don't see why he can't talk about it. After all, a grown actor plays the dinosaur…and adults produce the show. They're making a living as entertainment professionals, aren't they?" She had a point, which I bet she shared with Reid as they made the long trek up the freeway. I only wish the teacher would have heard her and creatively integrated it into the lesson plan for the next day.

Curbing a special interest to make it age appropriate is an art not a science. The goal should always be in the best interest of the child or developing teen, to help them reach their personal best.

It's not that we give a child whatever they want when its babyish or unhealthy, but that we work together to make progress and not stay stuck for posterity.

Sometimes clothing and accessory choices come into question in the name of age appropriateness. Reid chews a lot of things—from pillows to pencils—seeking proprioceptive input through his jaw. Rather than use baby teethers or a necklace around his neck, we encouraged gum chewing and even PVC pipe when it seemed more socially appropriate in his teens. It was in his best interest to fit in with his peers, yet we had to acknowledge his great need to bite something.

Unable to tie his shoes until recently, Reid was a fan of slip-on shoes. Over the years, he has sported Merrell Jungle Mocs, Vans Slip-Ons, and Crocs waterproof sandals in summer. At the end of an IEP meeting once, an administrator implored us in a peeved tone to please send him in different shoes. "Those Crocs make him stand out." This was the school whose expressed goal was to have the students blend in and go unnoticed in a crowd. While part of me relished the thought that he might some day fit in, I also shuddered at the impropriety of her suggestion. It smacked of conformity and standardization, especially delivered in the context of the rest of the meeting. Can I tell you we switched his placement from that school shortly after? Here's the clincher. The first day I dropped Reid off at the new school, the director himself was wearing Crocs! If the full-grown adult male in charge was sporting waterproof plastic shoes, then Reid could, too! I knew he was in the right place.

Whether choosing wardrobe, free-time activities, or workbook pages, we can customize a child's choices to grow with them and be age appropriate. Normal is overrated and situational. It's subtle, but I think you'll see how the goal of fitting in or fixing the child is distinctly different from coming alongside and helping him achieve a new personal best. Reid, and probably your child as well, can sense the difference. Usually the hard and fast rules are the ones that need to be reexamined for how and why they were laid down.

Intentionality and creativity are all it takes to adapt your student's special interest to their age and ability, keeping it relevant and educational. Take a peek at what same-age peers are doing on Facebook or in your neighborhood for ideas and a reality check. I once asked a friend with teenagers what their bedtime routine was like. She recounted it in detail for me, showing me that we weren't so far off base and that I didn't have to feel guilty for not exactly tucking Reid in every night. If you don't consider yourself creative, ask a friend or teacher to brainstorm with you and come up with a bunch of new ways to morph your child's special interest into their current stage of life. You don't have to do them all, just keep the list handy to keep you inspired that there is no end to the possibilities.

*How can your child's special interest grow with them?*

*Who is a new person who could expand your child's special interest?*

*What do your child's peers do that relates to your child's passion?*

# 8

*Playing from Memory*

## Play to the Strength

## *Playing from Memory*

*Countless piano teachers agree that memorization is beneficial. My fourth-grade piano teacher felt so strongly about it that she wouldn't let me advance a page in my book until I could play each song by memory. That seemed excessive for ditties like "Up and Down on the Seesaw" or "Floating Down the River." Nevertheless, playing by heart requires that the musician understands the music really well. Only then is he able to concentrate completely on the interpretation of the piece. To memorize music, students must learn a piece backward and forward. Only then they can perform it with fluency and freedom.*

*Doing what we were truly made to do is like playing from memory. While it requires practice and work, there is also a rightness or effortlessness to it when we find the sweet spot of natural gifting and purpose. Clara Schumann, the German composer, felt that playing by heart "gave her wings power to soar."*

# 8

## Play to the Strength

*I've never missed a gig yet. Music makes people happy and that's why I go on doing it. I like to see everybody smile.*

—BUDDY GUY

It is one thing to Teach to the Strength, the fifth principle. What I mean by Play to the Strength in this chapter is a combination of letting our kids use their natural gifts (as opposed to being an obstacle to them or hoping they might somehow develop different ones) and appreciating the strength even when it creates friction or other challenges. It is widely agreed that one's greatest strength can also be their greatest weakness. This is all the more true in our kids who may have strengths in excess, or at the expense of a more balanced neurology. Playing to the strength includes building an awareness of the pitfalls of the strength or special interest, curbing it when necessary, and identifying niche environments where it is appropriate and can develop. It also implies surrendering to what their purpose might be in life, however awkward or messy at times.

Reid loves to be in charge. When he was nine, we devised a game called "Navigator" that let him have a little of the control that he craved. Directionality, learning left from right, was an emerging goal at the time. We would get in the car on a Saturday morning and he would direct us which way to turn at every intersection. Jim was really in charge, of course. After a while, we realized Reid was literally mapping our community in his mind. He will never be lost; that much is sure. I used to say if there were any continents left to discover, he would find them. I often check with him if I am unsure which exit to take to a certain destination. He is always right. When Allie got her driver's license, she joked that she would have to take Reid along as her navigational system. She is a reliably capable and cautious driver, but could not always figure out where she was or how to get from here to there. He could.

A similar desire to understand the big picture is behind Reid's fascination with remotes, as distracting as it can be. Whenever he has access to a new television set, at a friend's house, a sports bar, or an unlocked conference room, he is compelled to explore the functionality of the remote. The owner or host might ask, "Can I help you? What are you looking for? Do you want Netflix?" Reid won't be interrupted at this task.

"It's not that," I usually interpret his lack of response. "He is not looking for any show in particular." Most often he is scoping out the entire site map, whether it is Apple TV, Comcast, or Infinity, and comparing it to ours at home. Holding a remote and "doing the honors," as he calls it, satisfies some of his craving to be in charge.

⸺ ᴄ ⸺

In short order, Reid became the self-appointed front man of the Kingsmen. Finally, it was socially acceptable for him to use his Activator and Command strengths. Many an Applied

Behavior Analysis (ABA)[9] specialist had attempted to extinguish these traits in him. Age-old compliance goals to stay in your seat, have quiet hands, and follow teacher instructions were the focus of much of his day and most of our conversations with school staff. Reid's behaviors were the greatest obstacle to his progress. In fact, the looming prerequisite of having him "under instructional control" obscured almost everyone's vision of what he might do in life. While I would have been happy to have him exhibit increased compliance, it is not a hallmark of leadership. Leaders don't typically follow directions blindly; they give the directions. That, he had mastered. Did he have control issues? Sure. Do most leaders? Yes.

What a relief it must have been for him to do what came naturally and not be corrected for it. Only then could he learn to curb his impulse to be the director and exercise what *StrengthsFinder* author, Tom Rath, calls "Ideas for Action" and "Working with Others" to develop his strength in healthy ways. Squelching his exuberance and innate strengths was not only *not* happening, it was also a misguided goal, in my opinion. Like working against the forces of nature to divert the ocean's force, pounding him for compliance was a lose-lose battle. "In six thousand years, you could never grow wings on a reptile," as the writer John McPhee put it.

─────ᶜ─────

There is a quintessential scenic drive near our home. Highway 101 comes within spitting distance of the Pacific Ocean, creating glorious views at sunrise, sunset, or in the fog. The coastal towns seem to battle

---

9 Applied Behavior Analysis (ABA) is the application of the principles of learning and motivation from Behavior Analysis, the scientific study of behavior, to the solution of problems of social significance.

nature in order to create prime real estate and viewing platforms along this stretch of land. Man attempting to curb the power of nature also seems a losing battle. Time and again, the ocean asserts itself and the developers must realign after a winter storm washes out yet another concrete esplanade or retaining wall designed to optimize the vista.

To me, these failed attempts are a picture of how strict ABA does our kids a disservice. In essence, it trains our kids to be rigid when they need to learn flexibility. Like reinforced steel, ABA is strong and should work, but it is no match for human nature, which includes a spirit and will. The father of ABA, Ivar Lovaas, and B. F. Skinner before him, were convinced that by forcing a change in a child's outward behavior, they could affect an inward psychological change. Deanne Shoyer[10] summarizes it well. "Skinner believed that human free will, human dignity, even human thought, were illusory. One of his primary goals was to devise methods for the control of human populations. Lovaas claimed he could have raised Hitler to be a nice person. Behaviorism has this tendency to deny, or at least underrate, human free agency and also genetics." While it has been softened and humanized since its abominable origins in the '60s, one needs to be wary of these unhealthy roots. We encountered people who claimed studying with Lovaas as a good thing on their resumes.

In our case, I grilled anyone using ABA principles to be sure their motives were in Reid's best interest, that they added and allowed for some heart in the protocols, and intentionally balanced it with more holistic, child-centered, empowering activities. Gratefully, we also found proponents of Pivotal Response Theory (PRT)[11] who had made their own departure from Discrete Trial

---

10 Deanne Shoyer writes about autism, neurodiversity, history, books, and apps at smallbutkindamighty.com

11 Pivotal Response Treatment is derived from ABA, but is play based and child initiated. It is one of the most validated behavioral treatments for autism and was developed by Lynn and Robert Koegel, PhDs at University of Santa Barbara.

Teaching[12] to incorporate more respectful therapies into their repertoire of services. As Reid changed schools in different seasons, we bumped into remnants of the rigid, nonfunctional, dehumanizing approach. He objected boldly, and while it took a little while for us to catch on, we were able to rescue him from the antiquated and even traumatic approaches.

ABA works in the short term and seems to be a necessary component of a quality program for kids on the spectrum, especially those with behaviors. In and of itself, though, it is not an education. I had a friend who was a curriculum writer. She came with me to an IEP at one school Reid attended. She was perplexed. "What curriculum are you using?" She asked the director several times during the meeting, "Where are the standards? I don't understand what you're actually teaching him. May I see the curriculum?" I was so used to their covert and inflexible approach I couldn't tell whether she was being unreasonable.

Days later it dawned on her like a bolt. "I figured it out. The behavior *is* the curriculum." That's all they were covering and Reid was a teenager at that point.

The other problem that occurs as a consequence of overusing ABA is what Alfie Kohn[13] refers to as being "punished by rewards." An ugly sort of entitlement results if our kids remain dependent on praise and rewards. I see it when Reid practices one song on the piano, then walks into the kitchen to tell me, "That deserves a reward." I heard it from him on our recent vacation. As we drove to the beach he needled us, "If I go to the beach, what do I earn?"

---

12 Discrete Trial Training is an adult-directed method of teaching that uses massed trial instruction, reinforcers chosen for strength, clear contingencies, and repetition to teach new skills and responses to stimuli.

13 Alfie Kohn is an educator who wrote *Punished by Rewards*, challenging behaviorists and advocating for teaching in context for a purpose.

At this point, accustomed to adjusting the home/school balance and using humor, we all burst out laughing. "Reid, this is supposed to be fun." We also knew he was lobbying for a trip to the bookstore, so we added, "Don't worry. We'll get to Mitchell's. That will be tomorrow's fun." He had been thoroughly trained to be extrinsically motivated, performing only for the prize. How could we cultivate his intrinsic motivation to do things for pure enjoyment or because they were good and right?

The aim of ABA is behavior modification, but as parents we might prefer to prioritize heart change and the transformation that flows naturally from there. Was that possible for kids on the spectrum? Was anyone doing it successfully? I ruminated over questions like these at length. Watching Reid repeatedly defy and test our limits brought me face-to-face with rebellion in my own life. In the midst of wondering why Reid would not simply obey, I had to admit there were ways I was giving my heavenly Father the same opposition and resistance that I was getting from Reid. I began to see myself in Reid, as well as empathize with God's role as the parent. I had to take a hard look at whether I really believed God loved me. Could I rest, be still, and receive his love? Or was I buzzing around trying to earn stickers on some celestial chart? Did I trust Him completely enough to do what He asked, even if it didn't make sense to me or I didn't feel like it? I began to see how these heart issues were at the root of my relationship with God and how my behavior flowed out of them.

Likewise, the more I convinced Reid that I loved him no matter what, and that he could trust me, the more his compliance and cooperation increased as a habit. When he was a mere seven, one of our more vested therapists had a similar moment of revelation. She confided in me that while waiting out one of his tantrums in a tight space, she was moved to tell him repeatedly, "I love you Reid.

I love you. I love you. I love you" in a soft, patient whisper. It was true; she did love him. (Reid senses people's true feelings toward him, perhaps more than most.) Her intuition told her that correcting this misbelief might be related to ending the tantrum that day. It didn't work instantly, but over time I think focusing on the heart rather than the outward behavior has shaped an alternative posture for him. I know it has for me, as a child of God.

I searched for verses that would lend a scriptural foundation to this issue that always caught in my spirit. Certainly, God established rules for our own good, in the form of the Ten Commandments. There are blessings as well as natural and spiritual consequences for either following or ignoring those — like a sticker chart. Beyond that, the Bible mentions rewards many times: "be strong and do not give up, for your work will be rewarded" (2 Chronicles 15); "love your enemies, do good to them, and lend to them… Then your reward will be great…" (Luke 6:35); and "God rewards those who earnestly seek Him" (Hebrews 11:6). Without question, God gives rewards even if we will be compelled to lay them all down at Jesus's feet when we experience Him face-to-face (Revelation 4).

On the other hand, our obedience or good works have no bearing on God's mercy. He offers all of us a free gift of love in His son. His grace is based on *His* faithfulness, not anything we do or fail to do. Was it a both/and? We had done both ABA and Floortime. Floortime has always been a picture to me of how Jesus came down to our level on earth, to meet us where we are and follow our lead just as the child-directed therapy defines.

Still, I knew there was more to it. While studying the theme of inheritance with Beth Moore, I got the real "Aha!" Every one of her Bible studies seems to parallel my life circumstance at the time and deliver God's word in a whisper to my ear. In *The Inheritance* she traces the theme of our inheritance as people of God, beginning in Genesis and threading its way through the entire Bible to Revelation. At the beginning, God tells Abram, "I am your shield, your very great reward!" (Genesis 15:1) More than any crowns in heaven or on earth, being in His presence, with Him, *is* the reward. The ultimate goal God has for each of us is personal intimacy with Him. Sounds like us that day at the beach, telling Reid, "Going to the beach with us *is* the reward!"

I got into a verbal standoff over rewards with one of Reid's more domineering shadow aides after high school one Friday. That day, or maybe the whole week, had been a long one. He had kept the requisite tally of maladaptive behaviors and was suggesting our weekly trip to the thrift store might be withheld as a penalty. I was irked; this was a clear case of separation of school and home, in my mind. He asked me, "How does Reid earn the thrift store?"

I looked him squarely in the eye, stating my policy, "We go because it's Friday."

I am more intentional now in striking a balance between the short-term effectiveness of behavior modification and the long-term relational benefits of learning more intrinsic motivation. We can reinforce even glimmers of that internalization through modeling and language. I ask Reid to clear his dishes after dinner because he's part of the family, rather than checking it off a chart for a sticker. Sometimes I buy him a cinnamon roll "because I love you" just to negate his need for tit for tat accounting. Admittedly, it can be a hard transition. We call him the "negotionator" because he knows all the best behavioral tactics; they were used on him.

If ABA is the foundation of a house, we must be sure to build something on top of it that is functional, fluid, comfortable, and visible, lest we live our entire life in the basement. Our kids, especially as they approach adolescence, need our help to build a future that flexes with them, suits the environment, and most important-ly, acknowledges their spirit.

—⸺

Without so much as a visual prompt, we watched Reid direct the sound check, count off the tempo, and keep the Kingsmen shows moving at an invigorating clip. The director tasks weren't ones you could teach his bandmates, nor did they want them. Like a drought-tolerant, indigenous native grass thriving in the hot California sun, he was in his element leading the band and getting the crowd go-ing. His famous tagline before every song was captured on their first recording. "Are ya ready, Charlie? Are ya ready, Conor?"

Repeated for each bandmate, it brought a chuckle from the audience, especially when the reply was, "Not yet, Reid." It was naturally occurring, real-world practice for "When Things Don't Go Your Way" (which is actually a song by Angela). More than once, the Kingsmen did a collective do-over. If they didn't all start together or a song was going off the rails, it was a good call to stop and start over. Goofing up was good practice for life. And they handled it, mostly on their own.

Teachers who came to his gigs were slightly dumbfounded. "Look at him up there. Oh my goodness." I don't think they had ever seen him so engaged or on point.

If we can identify a student's strengths with the help of *StrengthsFinder* and other tools, as well as define an area of special interest, then we can write better IEP goals. I am certain some por-tion of Reid's noncompliance was an attempt to lead. Focusing on deficits can become a misguided attempt to change our students at the very least, or control them at the worst. That must not be the point of education. The other unfortunate result of focusing on deficits is that we overlook the natural giftedness and raw talent that could be encouraged rather than extinguished. Playing to the strength offers an alternative.

Interestingly, to this day Angela has not witnessed Reid's most severe behaviors. She has been spared the impulsivity, outbursts, and aggression that gave me a coronary a day for a season. When she started playing piano, he shot to her side on the bench, the exact opposite of the wandering away he did everywhere else. If he were about to explode in frustration at not being able to find the right note, her musical response in another octave would hold it at bay. Such is the power of music in his life, as well as her skill using it. As long as music under-girds the activity, he is not pushed to the breaking point of melting down. In a very real sense, the music holds his fragile nervous system together, even restoring it from a frazzle on many occasions.

Reid's self-perception and identity changed during this season of Playing to his Strength. He announced, "I'm a musician." He invited friends to gigs and developed a sense of responsibility to be on time, stay motivated for a goal, and practice. Even on the nights he didn't want to go to practice, I would hear his self-talk. "The band needs me." The hardest thing was waiting for afternoon and evening gigs because he would be dressed, ready, and waiting in the car at 8:00 a.m. for an event that didn't start until after dinner. See, even time concepts can be taught through music!

Succeeding on stage, not to mention the concrete praise of the applause, developed Reid's awareness of how to behave appropriately off-stage. He began to transfer this success to daily life and other settings as we anchored and reinforced it for him. Doing the right thing and being successful was a refreshing tonic that built on itself.

The Kingsmen became de facto spokesmen for Banding Together, a music therapy nonprofit[14] Angela and I started to provide scholarships, instruments, and mentorships for youth with special needs. Standing before a crowd, the band is a living testimony of the outcomes and benefits of music therapy. In the process of playing at fund-raising events, the boys learned the concept of giving to others and helped raise money for the grassroots nonprofit. Seeing the powerful impact of music therapy in Reid's life motivated me to make it more accessible for kids like him. Whether it was hiring Angela to consult at his school or conceptualizing programs for the nonprofit, I was willing to do almost anything to bring more music into his life. If Reid could make music more days of the week and socialize with more people in the process, it was worth my investment of time and energy. I also knew that he was not unique. The music activities that worked for him continue to attract countless other families, especially when it is more affordable.

Banding Together's flagship program is a series of free, sixty-minute Jam Sessions[15] expertly facilitated by two music therapists. Each participant with special needs has a volunteer mentor who sits next to him and gets personally acquainted over the eight weeks. In addition to a drum circle time, thematic role-playing, and a turn at the microphone, each Jam Session includes a guest artist from the community who leads a song, answers questions, and interacts musically with the group. The structured flexibility of this musical encounter is adored by all the participants, including

---

14 Banding Together is a music therapy nonprofit with a mission to give scholarships, mentorships, and instruments to youth with special needs. BandingTogetherSD.org

15 The Jam Session program will be licensed and available to other music therapists in Spring 2016.

my husband who is one of the mentors. He has never had such a good reason to practice his guitar. Not surprisingly, there is a wait list for the program, since it meets a vital need for young adult social programs and is accessible to such a wide range of abilities. Music levels the playing field, so executives are able to interact with nonverbal autistics, enjoying every minute of it.

Reid is an active participant in these, as we predicted. Not only does he want to sing, drum, and dance, he is quite comfortable leading them. He struts in like a drum major with accentuated posture and leaves with the same adrenaline boost that he has after a gig. Language flows from him like an excited poet after a triple espresso. One night on the drive home we stopped by a convenience store for something. He came up with some doozies.

"That was spooky in there. If I bought those videos it would be a disaster." Those were unusual word choices for him at twenty-one.

I put down my phone and said, "Wow, Reid those are some impressive words you're using."

"Hey, Mom! I'm using a great vocabulary."

"Oh my gosh, I know. That's outstanding."

"Hey, you are too, Mom."

It struck me. Of course, we just left Jam Session. The musical activity hooked his brain up for higher functioning. Like an endorphin rush for a runner or a shot of steroids, music pumped him up so he was firing on all cylinders. It kept us going back for more.

―♪―

Reid's spirited, strong-willed personality demanded Playing to his Strength. I have observed that if something works for Reid, it's good for the rest of the class and the rest of the family, too. His intensity and complex needs have raised the bar for us as parents. He teaches the teachers in every setting he has visited, too. For most of his life, he has required exceptional babysitters, customized programs, top-notch dentists, progressive health care, and extraordinary neighbors. The rest of the family then benefits from the extra steps and information; we end up taking better quality vitamins, accessing alternative health care, expecting better protocols, or just boarding airplanes earlier. It can be a good thing for everyone to raise expectations and live on your toes, as it were. Your child may not assert himself as strongly, but trust me that this principle of Playing to their Strength will reveal potential and take them farther than you imagined.

Reid is about to complete the adult-transition program and exit the school district for good at age twenty-two. His teacher and I both welled up at his last annual IEP meeting as she highlighted his answers to a requisite student interview. What got her was his apology embedded in a reply to the question "When do you have problems during your school day?" She choked up reading it aloud, "When I bite myself. I'm sorry, Miss Catherine."

My eyes were drawn to a different one as I skimmed the bulky packet. Number seven, the last question on the same questionnaire, made me tilt my head and swallow a salty pout. It asked, "Is there anything else you'd like us to know about you?" Reid's answer: "I'm so smart because I play in a band." Indeed, it was important to add. Like glowing red brake lights on the freeway during a whiteout blizzard, if we keep our eyes on a special interest, following it hard, we will surely make it. After twelve years in the system, he had found a way to advocate for himself and hopefully those who would come after him with musical intelligence.

Musicians are gonna make music; leaders are gonna lead. Their innate strengths aren't likely to change that much. We saw this with Allie, too. The one season she ran cross-country, we drove to Coronado Island—an hour from home—for her first meet. Jim left his office early to make the two-hour trek to see her run. From the off-ramp of the bridge, we could see the meet already in process. As Jim searched for a parking spot, I squinted to identify Allie in the pack of runners. "Is that her?" Dead last, two girls went through the motions, just barely in the race.

Jim glanced. "I think so."

"What is she doing? Is she sick?"

We both knew she could run faster than that. It was puzzling as we hustled to the finish line, pretending we'd been there the whole time. Come to find out, her teammate thought she might throw up. Allie wanted to stay with her, running at the slow jog, so she wouldn't be alone feeling sick. Initially, we objected with comments like: "You know the point is to win, right?" "You need to run *your* fastest." "What'd the coach say?" And even "Let someone else watch her." In time, it became a picture of Allie's strengths: Adaptability, Includer, and Relator. Innately, in a way that cannot really be trained, she is a natural shepherd, coming alongside those in need, sacrificing her own gain in order to serve. No amount of money or bribery, in the form of Puma shoes or videotapes, would change this. And why would we want to? It is a beautiful thing the world needs.

Once you know your child's strengths (and your own), teach to them, and keep on playing to them. Look for ways to expand, develop, and employ both their special interest and their innate strengths. Help them choose activities that are conducive to their strengths. Introduce them in person, online, or through books, to others who have the same gift. Encourage them to share it with the world. I promise you it is where they will be most motivated and find the most purpose. It is how they were made.

*Where does your child absolutely shine (or have no behaviors)?*

*Where does your child get to exercise their innate gift?*

*Are the adults in your child's life working with him or against him?*

9

*Take a Master Class*

Cultivate Mentors

### Take a Master Class

*A master class is a class given by an expert to highly talented students of a particular discipline. Students and spectators watch and listen as the master engages with several selected students, one at a time. They take turns performing a piece they have prepared, then the master gives advice on how to play it better. He might share anecdotes about the composer, demonstrate how to play certain passages, offer tips on style and presence, or admonish technical errors. The student is expected to play the piece again, incorporating the master's comments. The audience learns by watching and listening, even if it is not their turn.*

*Allie and I sat together in the fourth row of a master class, watching the famous flutist, James Galway, with his flamboyant purple velvet suit, priestly cross pendant, and twinkling Irish eyes school the next generation. I don't even play flute, and I learned by watching him handle the audience at large, the three selected students, the stage, and his own instrument. Surrounded by the next generation of young, mostly female and Asian flute players, he imparted wisdom and freely shared all he knew in helpful doses, as mentors do.*

# 9

## Cultivate Mentors

*I wanna be like you-hu-hu*
*I wanna walk like you, talk like you, too.*
*You'll see it's true (Shoo-be-dee-doo)*
*Someone like me-e-e*
*Can learn to be*
*Like someone like you.*

—RICHARD AND ROBERT SHERMAN,
*THE JUNGLE BOOK*

Perhaps the best way to play to one's strength and foster a special interest is through mentoring. Watching and copying a master, in the old-world sense of apprenticeship, is so well suited to our students on the spectrum. It is concrete, visual, interactive, hands-on, kinesthetic, and often one-on-one, all the modalities and modifications that are proven best practices for ASD learners. The mentor need not be famous for their skill, only experienced at some skill the student has yet to master: conversation, pumping gas, making burritos, washing cars, affectionate arm poking, or using slang.

Temple Grandin says over and over again, "Mentors were pivotal to my success." She gives her science teacher, Mr. Carlock, credit for investing in her future by challenging, encouraging, and inspiring her. Of course, she met him and they connected based on their mutual special interest in inventing and experiments. We didn't set out to make Angela a mentor, but it certainly happened over time. As I mentioned, she was a welcome Friday-afternoon fixture in our home for years.

At dusk one evening during the Christmas season, a knock sounded at our door. I couldn't imagine who it could be. We had family in town and were gathered around the fireplace with glasses of merlot, preparing for a round of charades. It was Angela. She had stopped to deliver an envelope to Reid. As he opened it, she told us the story of an influential couple in her life who had given her her first recording session when she was in high school. She wanted to do the same for Reid as a Christmas gift now that he was sixteen.

We were moved by the gesture. She was coaching Reid through the next steps, showing him where music could take him. To use the gift and record a song meant they would have to collaborate and write their first original song "Shine." Writing one's own music opens new doors for recording and performing. Other bands could play Reid's pieces, and it was the natural progression for a musician. Learning the recording process would present a new challenge and show him another part of the business. All these endeavors distinguish musicians from students. Not that I knew that; Angela was teaching me, too.

Prior to this, Angela had organized GarageBand camps for the Kingsmen where they recorded themselves and learned the basics of that software with help from local musicians. Going to an actual recording studio with a producer took this to the next level. Reid would be following the producer's directions, showing respect for equipment, and recording vocal tracks while listening to the piano track in headphones. These were all new skills scaffolded by familiarity, structure, his intrinsic motivation, as well as Angela's presence.

A few years later, Angela invited Reid to be the guest musician at her Camp Jam program, a day camp for younger children with special needs. Reid was to be the closing act of a music-filled day. The campers presented coupon "tickets" to attend his show and practice polite audience manners of listening and clapping. Reid naturally emulated what he had seen Angela do for years, taking on a junior therapist role and copying the guest artists he had seen at the Jam Sessions. This took his leadership skills up a notch and enabled him to use his natural bent and simpatico for Angela to serve others, work on vocational goals, and even earn some money.

At one of these Camp Jams, there was a boy named Freddy who was overwhelmed by the commotion of ten other campers and their volunteer aides. In order to cope with the chaos, Freddy clasped his hands over his ears. When we arrived, he and his aide were taking a break in the relative solace of the room where Reid was to warm up. We couldn't miss Freddy careening about the room, vocalizing his frustration with screams and grumbling while the other children did a craft in another room. He reminded me of Reid at that age trying to escape a noisy restaurant.

Honestly, I was nervous that Reid might do what I had seen him do in the past, namely match Freddy's distress or raise it a decibel. Instead, in a marker of maturity, he kneeled to address him. "Freddy, it's OK. Don't scream. Take a deep breath." Then he proceeded to the keyboard. "Quiet now, I'm going to play a song just for you." And he did. He ran through his set list, and Freddy quieted down. It was a reprieve for everyone; music saved another day. When the rest of the campers began to file in, Freddy had to switch rooms again to find an empty one, but he hadn't missed out entirely. He had gotten a private show.

Reid's empathy had developed full circle. Ten years prior, he had been Freddy. Many times after grueling days at school, music had been a healing balm and reset button for him. As he hobbled off the bus, I felt helpless to redeem his demanding day of behavioral correction, but exceedingly grateful on the days Angela showed up. Thirty minutes with her was like a reboot. She might play a song that matched his energy, suggest a blues exercise on piano or a movement song that would literally shake the strain off, as only music can do. Truly, "music has charms to sooth a savage breast, to soften rocks, or bend a knotted oak," as William Congreve wrote in Shakespeare's day. It helped Reid remember life was worth living.

"The delicate balance of mentoring someone is not creating them in your own image, but giving them the opportunity to create themselves," is how Steven Spielberg put it. The mentoring continues, as Reid and Angela just released their first full-length CD. *Purple Party* is a collection of catchy songs about each color of the rainbow: "Red Song by Reid," "Orange Piano," "Mellow Yellow," "Being Green," "I've Got the Blues," and the title track, "Purple Party." They collaborated in the true sense of the word, Angela choosing chords, Reid throwing a lyric into the ring, and then hashing and refining them over weeks together. Once we had the full spectrum of songs, we decided to release them as an album. Reid participated fully in the recording process with Angela, a local drummer, and several graduates of Berklee College of Music, the prestigious school Allie now attends. We planned it when she was home to play flute on several of the tracks, and producer Chris Hobson is an alumnus. Would you believe, Allie's friend, Emma Byrd, happened to be interning with Angela over the course of the recording sessions, making the Berklee connection a majority? She carried kazoo and bass parts with panache. Reid has known the drummer, Brian Dall, since that first gig at the NBC Plaza when he came up to his knees in their matching maroon T-shirts and jeans. Brian is practically an honorary Kingsmen, having taught the drummer and played in on numerous occasions. The thirty-hour recording process ensured the professionalism of *Purple Party* and made them all mentors to Reid. "If you're going to make music, make sure it's good," is Angela's first songwriting tip on the bonus track.

⎯⎯᪥

Mentors are important for moms, too. When we returned to San Diego with five-year-olds, our new pediatrician introduced me to two moms whom she admired as passionate advocates for their boys. I called them both and clicked with one. For fifteen years, Shawn and I shared many of the same nannies, tutors, preschools, private teachers, therapists, and brainstorms. We had the same mindset toward our circumstances and similar expectations for our boys. Our boys' paths intersected as we crisscrossed the county, finding the best ways for them to plug in and comparing notes at every juncture. We became Kingsmen roadie moms together and enjoyed that wild ride. Shawn made me better by caring, challenging, always thinking ahead, and being another champion for Reid.

Facing the same daily battles, we also knew we could call each other at any time and unload, which we did. I remember as if they were historic events, the exact place and time of some of our conversations when we each in turn faced a med change, a marriage crisis, or a new discovery. If you don't have a mentor friend like Shawn, ask your doctor for one, seriously.

One of Reid's earliest home-program supervisors, who we shared with Shawn, was also a mentor as we began the early intervention treadmill. I made it a point to watch and learn from all Reid's early therapists, since I wanted to integrate the therapy into our lives. Janelle was particularly accessible to me, listening as I processed our new status aloud. At one point, observing my fervor, she counseled me, "I feel like you're treating this like a sprint, but it's a marathon, so you need to run it as such. You're not going to make it at this pace." It was good advice I pass on to you.

I wasn't particularly good at the self-care that is advisable for moms in our boat. I tended to bite the head off anyone who suggested, "You should take care of yourself. Do something fun once in a while." It felt like that added one more impossible task to my exhaustive list of how to help Reid catch up to his peers before he reached age six…or eight…or… To be told that if you do enough intensive intervention and keep them engaged every waking minute, you might be able to bring your child out of their autism or diminish the symptomology is an incredible, looming responsibility and burden already. I resented the suggestion that I might be failing in one more way.

I declined retreats because the regular childcare never worked for us. Support groups seemed depressing to me, like clinging to another drowning victim in a riptide. While misery loves company, they didn't do much to edify or elevate any of us. Sometimes it foretold issues that might not go away, but get worse.

Moms groups and even Bible studies were often alienating because my scenario was so unusual I couldn't share it without shocking the poor other ladies. My prayer requests seemed to trump the others, and I wasn't comfortable dominating or shutting down the sharing time. When everyone else was praying for their daughter's first dance recital, it didn't seem fair to bring up Reid's gastrointestinal issues. I didn't like being the squeaky wheel.

I'm an introvert, so alone time, like a walk on the beach or browsing a bookstore served me better. What also fed me was a good book that inspired me to greatness or overcoming obstacles. I read an entire stack of Lance Armstrong biographies, which seems oddly appropriate now.

One-on-one time, sharing heart to heart with another mom in a waiting room also fortified me for the next day and advanced my knowledge of whatever therapy our kids were engaged in behind the closed door. When the Kingsmen gathered, we enlarged that ratio to four moms in a waiting room laughing and connecting while the boys rehearsed. In truth, my closest friends were those who loved Reid as much as I did. Instead of "love me, love my dog," I guess I lived by the motto, "Love Reid and I can spend time with you." That was our reality.

My closest friend—really we're sisters at this point—was one of Reid's original home tutors. He and I both fell in love with Carla. Her playful positivity coupled with Strategic, Communication, and Relator strengths were a match made in heaven. Ten minutes of watching her do Floortime with Reid, and I wanted to join them. It energized me to be around someone who loved him so wholeheartedly and was good at what we needed most. When I was most depleted or burned out, watching a superb therapist genuinely enjoy my child rejuvenated me vicariously. Find those people who model what you want to be with your kids, make them mentors, and get an injection of them frequently.

Carla has a long list of "firsts" with Reid, including using a computer mouse, writing his name, being a sheep in the Christmas pageant, and sleeping away from home. As she moved away and started her own family and coaching business, she continues to mentor me in writing and marketing. Who knew way back when how permanent she would be in our life? Like manna, God has provided wonderful people at pivotal times to be intensely involved in our journey. Then, also like manna, they go away and a new intervention or chapter begins with someone else. His provision tends to arrive just when you need it and stays only as long as you need it. I've been amazed more than once when tutors, teachers, and even neighbors have circled back into our lives in a new capacity at a different stage. Some have become friends rather than employees; others are newly minted administrators playing a vital role in our community, still pouring into Reid's life in a fresh, yet familiar, way.

I may as well throw in another thing not to do. I tried to be everything to everyone until Reid was in about fourth grade when I literally said, "Enough." Out of desperation one Sunday, I quit my post as a volunteer Sunday school teacher, though I had been in Reid and Allie's classroom every year since they had entered the nursery. I signed up with a passionate insistence that Reid be included (and not be a burden to anyone). My heart was for the handful of challenging kids who couldn't quite hack Sunday school. I told the coordinator, "Give me the tough ones. I'll find a way to teach them." I think subconsciously, I was still trying to prove that I was a good mom; the residual shame and unworthiness of infertility and adoption issues lingered. But after six years, it approached the absurd and ridiculous. Reid would leave the classroom, wander the campus, and no one but me noticed, let alone retrieved him. On that last Sunday, I couldn't find Reid anywhere. Pacing the campus frantically, I bumped into the supervisor and threw up my hands. "I can't do this anymore." It was the truth. Why someone hadn't fired me sooner, I am not sure. I never taught another Sunday school class. The point being: you don't have to do it all.

Perhaps the most powerful self-care strategy I learned the hard way, by failing at it repeatedly. It is to be what Psalm 1 calls "like a tree planted by streams of water." Understandably, my mood and outlook were often determined by how Reid's day went. There is a very real temptation, more like a magnetic pull, to let our kids become the center of our universe. It is almost inevitable given the constancy and urgency of their extensive needs. Add unpredictable behavioral incidents to the mix, not to mention the copious analyzing and troubleshooting that goes with it, and you have a veritable path of hot coals to walk over before you get into bed each night.

In time and with practice, I learned to extend my roots down deeper to something permanent and immovable where soothing water was plentiful and I could "yield fruit in season and…not wither." Knowing an unchanging God better, and more personally, gave me staying power and the assurance that someone was in control of the seemingly random outbursts. As I drew sustenance from God, I was able to take things in stride and not let Reid's tough days set me so far back each time. God is a better anchor than any child.

I have another mentor and kindred spirit in Sandi, who I met when Reid was about twelve, just in time to walk us through the awkward years. A creative encourager, she charts a course for many moms in this region. Her entrepreneurial son, Joel Anderson, was also featured on the Songstream Project "Voices of Autism" show. His business, Joel's Vision Arts, is thriving as he pursues his passion for painting and animation to make the world a better place. I call Sandi when I am stymied or discouraged, and she gives me at least five good ideas per conversation. Joel is four years older than Reid, so she is one curve ahead of us on the journey and keeps me prepared for the next thing.

"Being a mentor is a brain to pick, an ear to listen, and a push in the right direction," as politician John Crosby said. Go and find a friend like Sandi who will encourage and challenge you. We share a special interest—our boys—and her strengths of creativity, resourcefulness, encouragement, and optimism rub off on me whenever we talk. The best mentors, in my opinion, do what Sandi does. She listens and hears me out, then she is able to speak the truth in love. Often that means saying, "Wait a minute. Stop thinking that way. You know that's not true. Let's get back on track and think this way." When it gets dark, she reminds me what I knew in the light.

At the same time Joel is a role model for Reid, modeling how to run a business, speak publicly, and advocate for himself. Watching Joel do address a crowd, exhibit his artwork, and be productive raises the bar on what Reid expects of himself. In a natural, yet revolutionary move, Reid hired Joel to design the custom coloring pages that accompany each of the songs on *Purple Party*. One young man with autism hired another, mutually employing their special interests; hopefully, that's a sign of the future. Downloadable from Reid's website, the coloring pages provide an extension activity for kids of any age. Although I am sure it won't be the last, in many ways the *Purple Party* CD is the culmination of Reid's life of music therapy. With it, he is using music to teach nonmusic skills (colors) to young children, the very thing Angela and others did for him.

⎯⎯⎯⎰⎯⎯⎯

Music therapy is a board-certified profession. Like speech therapy and occupational therapy, it requires a college degree, five practica in various settings, an internship akin to student teaching, and a certification test. Music however, is simple and accessible enough for anyone with a voice to use it therapeutically, which is what makes it so versatile and transferrable for mentoring. During Reid's teenage years, we met Tobias Haglund and helped him bring Young Life Capernaum,[16] a faith-based ministry to youth with special needs, to San Diego. In his commitment and passion for relationships, Tobias made it his practice to come to our house and worship with Reid once a week.

It may surprise you to hear what an awkward adjustment this was for all of us. Tobias arrived with no agenda. He was unpaid and willing to stay longer than a clinical hour. At first, Reid did not necessarily welcome the visit, even if Tobias did have a guitar. He didn't comprehend the goal, and I wasn't sure whether to insist he join Tobias on the sofa or let it be optional. After more than a decade, it was a definite shift to approach music recreationally with a nontherapist. Once we sorted out the nuances, this became a treasured time of the week. Overhearing the naturally occurring time of two guys just hanging out, singing together was profound for me. From a three-ring binder of chord charts, they would pick five songs each and sing them at the top of their lungs. In the middle, they'd post a selfie on Instagram and sometimes place a speakerphone call to Tobias's fiancé. We all crave ritual.

Music provided the structure Reid needed to support a social interaction. Eventually, he and Tobias took their music time on the road to a local group home and served others with music. In this way, Tobias became another mentor. Especially for adolescents, having objective, third-party, outside influences is vital to the mental and emotional health of everyone in the household. It

16 Young Life is a Christian ministry that reaches out to middle school, high school, and college-aged kids in all fifty United States and more than ninety countries. Capernaum is dedicated to programs for students with disabilities. YoungLife.org

is developmentally appropriate for teens to hear input from adults who are not their parents, and for us to relinquish some control and let them practice independence safely with supervision.

As Jim and I watched Tobias with Reid, we both adjusted to the new terrain of having an adolescent son. Seeing Reid interact with a typical male role model was a marked contrast to the years of female therapists and caregivers; it was eye opening and aspirational. Seeing him side by side with Tobias who was twenty-something, redefined our expectations of what was "typical" for Reid as he approached his twenties. As a friend and mentor to Reid, Tobias was actually giving Jim new ideas and ways to engage with our growing son.

This is one of the frequently sited benefits of the Autism Tree Project Foundation[17] Football Mentorship program. Players from the San Diego State University Aztec team are matched up with families and interact with them in caring ways throughout the football season. Parents report that for many, it is the first activity their husband has been interested in doing with their autistic child. Unlike therapy, they don't have to be trained in a whole new skill set, videotaped, and evaluated. They can just be themselves and enjoy time with their son. This is a liberating invitation for a lot of dads, and hanging out with college football players is an added enticement. They receive something from the experience of having their son or daughter accepted, and it fuels acceptance and love in their own actions. Mentorships, in music or sports, expand the social possibilities for our students and their families.

When it came time for Reid's high school graduation party, he handwrote the guest list for me. At the top were all the

---

17 Autism Tree Project Foundation is a nonprofit dedicated to assisting with education, advocacy, early intervention preschool screening, and mentoring for families impacted by autism. AutismTreeProject.org

worship leaders, music teachers, and guitar-playing pastors we knew. Following those were names of his same-age peers and some family friends. We let Reid plan and direct the whole party. He greeted each guest with panache, walking out to the curb like a valet and escorting them from the street. The five musicians who came were enlisted when it came time for the "show." Reid and his company of mentors led the rest of the guests in an unrehearsed concert of his favorite worship songs. Then he recruited a brave, unsuspecting girl to do a solo of Pharrell Williams's song "Happy." It was everything he envisioned: to be surrounded by those people he admired and demonstrate how much he'd absorbed by watching them. One of them who hadn't seen Reid in a while was astonished. "I can't believe it. He's a natural up there, telling us what to play, getting everyone situated, and prompting the next lines. He knows exactly what he's doing."

Nodding, all I could say was, "He's learned from the best!"

After the structured "gig" part, Reid returned to watching videos. He didn't see the point or enter into the process of milling about with food on plates. He had had his moment. He ate after everyone left and the house was quiet again. To each his own.

I don't think it's possible to have too many mentors. Some are paid, some unpaid. Some you ask, others just appear. Some are forever, others just a little while. They all inspire us to grow. Mentors come in many shapes and sizes, ages and stages. They might be closer than you think. Look around and notice who takes an interest in your child and what they can do. Who are the people your child assimilates with or aspires to be like? They might enjoy spending time modeling their skill and passing it along to your son or daughter. There is no substitute for mentoring; it synthesizes book learning and direct instruction, making it three dimensional in real time. It is relational—someone to be with—rather than just something to do.

*Who does your child gravitate to as a mentor or hero?*

*Who shares your child's special interest and enjoys spending time with them?*

*Where can your child pass along what they know?*

# 10

*Dissonance Seeks Resolution*

## Siblings Can Thrive

## Dissonance Seeks Resolution

*Dissonance is an unstable sound of notes that may express pain, grief, and conflict. The tension of dissonant chords demands an active, onward motion toward a stable consonance. The move from dissonance to consonance provides resolution in music.*

*Dissonance, suspense, and resolution create musical interest. Even harmonious music incorporates some degree of dissonance. The buildup and release of tension is part of what listeners perceive as beauty, emotion, and expressiveness in music.*

*In life difficulty and trials, or dissonance if you will, define us and give us beautiful stories to tell. The unpleasant challenges make us wiser, more resilient and confident to face the rest of life. A child with special needs can create a dissonant childhood for those near him, but often the resolution is a strong conviction or calling that could only be forged in that crucible.*

# 10

## Siblings Can Thrive

*A person comes into the world with a fist and a grasp. Yes,
we are built to fight one another, but also to embrace. How
cleverly we are created.*

—RACHEL SIMON, AUTHOR OF *RIDING THE BUS WITH
MY SISTER*

I'd be lying if I said I never worried about Allie. As parents consumed with special needs kids, part of the invisible tattoo we share is the constant concern that we are neglecting our other children. As common as that is, so is the incredible character that results from growing up with a sibling who has special needs. I can list (and would like to hear them on a well-facilitated panel) the adults I know whose skills and specialty were born out of being and having an exceptional sibling: Angela Neve, Alan Lincoln, Joan Hewitt, Adryon Ketcham, Diana Pastora-Carson, Rachel Simon, Matt Asner, Maria Shriver, Glenn Close, Michael Caine, Arthur Miller, Allie Moriarty.

I used to routinely inquire of our home tutors and new staff, "How did you get into this work?" Consistently, the best ones had an answer related to their own struggles or those of a sister or brother in their formative years that—more than any training or certification—gave them invaluable empathy, insight, experience, and passion to truly make a difference.

Someone recently asked Reid, "Who is your childhood hero?"

He paused, considering his options, then said, "Well, someone in the family…I think Allie is my hero."

It's true. He looks up to Allie and has learned the most from her. She has, "in the face of adversity, displayed courage and self-sacrifice for the greater good," which defines a heroine. Together from conception, they have arguably taught each other everything they know, or at least learned it all in tandem. This makes it tricky for Allie to answer essay questions like, "Describe the first time you encountered someone with a disability." She's never *not* known one. It was all she knew, yet she didn't really think of Reid as "disabled" until she reached middle school. Surely, as twins, they were each other's closest friend, and because she could do everything before him, she was his role model for every developmental milestone from walking to talking to changing schools to moving out of the house. They shaped each other and carry each other with them.

When Allie and Reid were about five years old and Reid's home program was in full swing, Allie asked me a recurrent question, "Mom, when will Reid play with me?"

Break a mother's heart, right? I honestly did not know how to answer her; I totally felt her pain. The same nagging question was stuck on my mind like a wad of gum to my shoe on a muggy day. We were doing everything humanly possible to help Reid engage and do what kids do at five years old, namely play. She logged in hours of failed attempts, and at times, it must have felt like all the adults around her, including me, weren't playing with her either. They were too absorbed in getting Reid to play.

In hindsight, I see how she found her answer. She studied the countless professionals who came through the house to successfully garner Reid's attention. Then she copied what they did. Her resolve to play with her twin brother was that strong, a primal motivator. Suffice it to say, she has serious skills. I recall a time when my mom came to stay with Allie and Reid for a week while Jim and I were out of town. She attempted to keep up our homeschooling regimen. When we touched base by phone, she was frustrated.

"Oh Andrea, I tried everything I could think of. I could not get Reid to do a thing." She felt like a failure. "Allie finally took over. She said sweetly, 'Here, Natty, let me try.' Then, she got him to do all his work. Honestly, I couldn't believe it. I was amazed." My mom taught second grade for twenty years, so she was no slouch. Special education is a definite specialty, and Allie was a master at eight years old.

Still, I will admit to wishing, in waves, that life were different for her. Well-intentioned friends and family fed into this, suggesting we create more of her own space or give her a break from the stress of having so many behaviors and chaos at home. "Wouldn't she be better off at a preschool five days a week?" or, "How is she doing with 'all this'?" were standard questions from the neighbors, referring to the neglect they assumed was inevitable with such a high-maintenance sibling.

On a good day, my best reply was, "I am trusting God to use 'all this' to equip and prepare her for something only she can do." I clung to that wishful thinking laced with true faith. "It won't be wasted. He put them together, and He knows what He is doing." I never pictured exactly what that would be, but I put my trust out on a limb. At the same time, I prayed she wouldn't pick a demanding, high-maintenance husband just because it was a familiar dynamic.

Around the time Allie entered middle school and had loads of homework in the afternoons and evenings, Reid began talking out loud to himself, addressing Allie in conversation. At first, this seemed odd. Jim would tell him, "Allie's upstairs. Go up there if you want to talk to her."

To which Reid replied, "I'm not talking to the real Allie. I'm talking to Allie-in-the-tummy." Allie-in-the-tummy was a sort of Jiminy Cricket–like conscience who listened to his thought process and helped him make decisions. Just like the real Allie, she had endless patience and always offered good advice. As Allie got her driver's license and eventually left for college, Reid carried her with him as this Allie-in-the-tummy. They consulted frequently, usually comparing the right thing to do versus what he wanted to do. She kept him company and helped him while he waited for his body to cooperate with his better judgment.

"Allie, I don't want to go to bed." Reid sat on the love seat in our living room. He was in his jammies, brushed and flushed as we say, but wanted to watch all the videos he had purchased at the thrift store that day. The rest of us were upstairs ready to shut 'er down. Even in the dark from the top of stairs, I could see the wheels turning inside his head. Nothing I might say or do would help. Sometimes he would even hold up a finger to shush me. "Mom, I know. I know. I'm doing it." He had to talk this through. I had best let him process the undesirable direction, weigh the pros and cons out audibly, and arrive at the right decision willingly.

"But Reid, you have to. Listen to what Mom said." His voice was higher and sweeter when he impersonated Allie.

"I want to watch *all* my movies right *now*." The debate went on with his characteristic insistence.

"I know Reid, but it's bedtime. You have school in the morning." Allie-in-the-tummy understood and acknowledged his feelings.

"How 'bout this? What if I rewind them tonight, then I could watch one before school?"

"You know the rules, Reid: No television before school. You could rewind them though." He stacked the tempting VHS tapes on the coffee table carefully aligning the edges until they were perfectly square.

"I don't know. Why not I stay up all night and watch them while Mom and Dad sleep?"

"I don't think so Reid. That's a bad idea. You need your sleep." Both Allies were so rational.

"Reeeallly...? But Allie, I want to watch them all." He was whining now, grimacing and pounding his fist for impact.

"Reid, listen to me. You can watch them after school tomorrow." Boy, he knew the drill and Allie could be firm. They were putting me out of a job.

"Okay, Allie! That might just work." He was pleased with himself now, removing his hands from the videos and standing up. Phew! My head was getting heavy. Allie's light was off.

"Good job, Reid. Now let's go up to bed." He bounded up the stairs and passed me with a cheery, "Goodnight, Mom. See you in the morning."

Another time, when he was about fourteen, Allie and I overheard Reid having both sides of a conversation while doing his independent homework problems at the kitchen table. He picked up a photo of himself that was propped on the centerpiece.

"Reid, you're adorable," he said in his Allie-in-the-tummy voice.

Then, as himself, correcting her gently, "I know, Allie, but let's get back to work."

We all have these two-way conversations with ourselves; they are just usually silent. *I'd like to eat this whole cake. No, I shouldn't. It's too many calories. Maybe just a bite. OK, that's enough. Now put it away.* Reid's relationship as a twin gave me an easy way to explain how we hear from the Holy Spirit. He is inside us, convicting, reminding, and encouraging us just like Allie-in-the-tummy. We have to learn to recognize his voice, discern which one is his, and then do as he is prompting. To be such a constant source of encouragement and good counsel does makes Allie "the best sister in the world," as Reid often calls her.

When she left for college, I think Allie was ready for a break from special needs. Following in the footsteps of two favored music teachers, she was clear in her desire to study music education. She loved Boston and Berklee College of Music, where everyone was a musician. After two years of conscientious study, she told me she was thinking about changing her major to music therapy. "Would you pray about it?"

Maybe this is the most obvious thing in the world now, but at the time it wasn't. I did pray, and as often happens, the prayer morphed as it was leaving my lips. I told her, "I don't think the prayer is 'Should you change your major?' I think it is 'Why are you resisting this?' If I were God and I wanted to create an incredible music therapist, I'd give someone your life."

She saw it then, too, and decided to complete a double major in music therapy and music education. She arrived at Berklee with skills that can't be taught in classrooms or practica, but only over the course of a lifetime in close, loving range of someone with special needs. To me, her coursework seems like therapy in itself, reflecting on her childhood and retelling it with new awareness of its application. Assignments like "How language development can be supported with music therapy" and "Document the pros and cons of including special learners in classrooms" read like a pages from our family scrapbook.

Now we see the plan that was meant to be all along. Would you like to know all of Allie's strengths? Includer, Developer, Relator, Adaptability, Responsibility. The *StrengthsFinder* tool gave me language to express the fulfillment of that faithful wish I had defensively proclaimed to the neighbors. All those awkward moments that onlookers worried would ruin Allie, in fact, forged her strengths. Politician Frank A. Clark said, "If you find a path with no obstacles, it probably doesn't lead anywhere." Her path has led to a specific passion for elementary-age children to accept and include their peers who are different in schools and classrooms. I think she is well equipped to make a dent in that noble mission with credibility and compassion.

In addition to believing the additional strain will work together into something good, there are specific ways we tried to compensate Allie for the inevitable times she drew the short straw. For many years, Jim and I alternated taking her on a Saturday breakfast date. It was a time she could count on our undivided attention. Jim drove her thirty minutes every day to her high school and cherished that time for conversation and playing deejay. Taking turns, she introduced Jim to the classical music she knew from playing in the San Diego Youth Symphony, and Jim exposed Allie to many of the eclectic and obscure bands that he follows. Music may have begun as a therapy, but it became bonding glue that held us together.

Learning your children's love language[18] can be a good way to make sure you are giving love in a currency they can receive. Allie's love language is Quality Time so sitting in her room at bedtime, whether or not we talked at all, was a way I could refill her love tank after long days. I had to be intentional about this, though, since my love language is Acts of Service. I actually think the landscaper is flirting with me if he offers to carry grocery bags in from my car. From my prerogative, I might assume that if I have fed and washed someone, scheduled their dentist appointment every six months, and made their bed, they would feel loved. Not necessarily. Those services in my love language don't equate to feeling loved in Allie's language of Quality Time. I learned to express love in different ways especially for her.

Outstanding therapists and teachers are mindful of ways to include siblings and take an intentional interest in them, lest they falsely conclude that the world revolves around their special needs sibling. When Allie was a kindergartner, many of Reid's tutors made a point of knowing her name, including her in therapeutic play, recognizing her birthday, and taking a few extra minutes at the door with her. If therapists don't do this automatically, ask them to.

When Angela taught Allie's flute lessons, they had their own private time. She was a mentor and role model to Allie as well as Reid as she shared the story of her brother with Angelman syndrome.

---

18 *The 5 Love Languages*® by Gary Chapman is a *New York Times* bestseller that has transformed countless relationships. It outlines five ways to express and experience love: gifts, quality time, words of affirmation, acts of service, and physical touch.

"When I got to school, I was surprised to learn that other people didn't have a brother like mine. I thought every family had someone with a disability," she shared. Never in long lectures but naturally over time, Allie knew that Angela understood our family dynamic, whether it was the way she held her eye contact and didn't allow Reid to interrupt a conversation, gave grace when we were late, or laughed at the same jokes recalling the awkwardness of middle school band class. Of course, in her very career choice, Allie continues to have a role model in Angela. She is a ready example of how to incorporate your life experience into purposeful adulthood, run a business, develop talent, and serve families.

Another way we made up for the unfairness of life was to apologize to Allie when autism seemed to rob her of a quiet bedtime ritual, a clean bathroom, or the whole family present at her graduation. It wasn't fair; we could be honest about that. At the same time, she wouldn't want to trade places with Reid, do his therapies, or go to his schools, so we reminded her to be grateful for the opportunities and gifts she had. In the end, our faith positioned us to be people of grace who looked for ways God would redeem our circumstances. Embracing His will over our own is a lifelong process that we modeled transparently for her in fits and starts.

Whatever potential damage the strain of having a special needs child places on your marriage or siblings in the household, there is an upside. Let it take its course and do its work; adversity does build character. "A sidekick helps the hero fulfill his destiny," is the beautiful way Pulitzer Prize–winning author Ron Suskind expressed it. Sometimes it is hard to tell which is which; sidekick and hero are so interdependent. Be honest about the demands, respond in specific loving ways, and most of all be open to the opportunity embedded in the challenge.

*How can members of your family grow, not in spite of, but because of the demands inherent with your special learner?*

*What is each of your children's love language (Quality Time, Acts of Service, Words of Affirmation, Gifts, or Physical Touch)?*

*What have you learned from dissonance, pain, or challenges in your own life?*

# 11

*Busking Out of Doors*

## Generalize Every Skill Everywhere

## Busking Out of Doors

*Busking refers to singing, making music, or dancing on the street or in a public place, usually while soliciting money. The motivation for doing street performance is to bring music to people who normally wouldn't hear it or can't afford a ticket. It is also a good way to get honest feedback from a crowd of people who don't know you or owe you anything.*

*Generalizing skills is like taking them on the road to see if they have been fully mastered outside the clinic or therapy session with people who are not specially trained or particularly acquainted with your child's particular needs and modifications. As in busking, it can be a reality check to enter a brand-new context, offering perspective to both the performer and the audience.*

# 11

# Generalize Every Skill Everywhere

*If I can make it there, I'll make it anywhere. It's up to you,
New York, New York.*

—Frank Sinatra

Functioning at your full potential in different settings or with different people can be tricky for students on the spectrum. Often our children are able to do a task one day with one instructor but cannot access that same skill another day or with a different person. Generalizing skills needs to be an intentional effort to practice and promote. Music is particularly easy to generalize across settings. As with other special interests, it can be the bridge that links the student from one instructor to another and one environment to another.

When he was about nine, Reid wanted to be in a local youth theater production. They required an audition. *Hmmm, what to sing?* He picked Angela's greeting song, since it was in his repertoire at the time. He had "Ways to Say Hello" in the can, as they say, even if it was an unconventional choice. It was a perfect opportunity to generalize his music, language, and presentation skills from

Angela's session to a welcoming, yet intimidating setting of brand-new, unsuspecting people. Allie and I sat in the front row, whispering about whether to bail or let Reid go through with this daunting experience. He sat (and paced back and forth) on the other side of the room near the row of chairs designated for about seventy other elementary-age students waiting to audition.

"I don't think they'll let me go up with him, do you?" I thought aloud.

"No, Mom, you cannot. I would never do this." Allie was mortified just having to wait and watch from our seats. We sat as close as we possibly could.

"Me neither, but he *wanted* to," I reminded her I was not forcing him to do this.

We were both beet red anticipating his turn, embarrassed vicariously. Allie slunk down in her chair trying to disappear behind my shoulder. I would've crawled under the seat except that, you know, I am a grown woman. We sat paralyzed, eyes forward, willing it to end well.

The room filled behind us with other spectators. Then, after what seemed a torturous amount of waiting, talented children belted out show tunes from all our favorite musicals. Reid mouthed the words to most of the songs: "Be Our Guest" from *Beauty and the Beast*, "The Bare Necessities" from *The Jungle Book*, and "A Whole New World" from *Aladdin*. A new worry emerged that he might sing along aloud disrupting another kid's moment, but he didn't.

They called his name. He bolted up to a woman taking notes at a table, operating the boom box. She was like home base in the ninth inning of a tied game. He clung to her with a monkey grip through the entire song, which masked his trembling knees. Whether it was endearing or inappropriate, I wasn't sure. No one pried him off her. As he finished his educational tune, complete with hand motions for the high five and handshake, the crowd of spectating parents and other contestants erupted into applause and sprung to their feet. It startled Allie and I out of our frozen state in the front row, but Reid was the real deer in the headlights. I will never forget their spontaneous ovation that day. Like the "cloud of witnesses" described in Hebrews 12, they were cheering us on to "run with perseverance the race marked out for us." Afterward, someone told me, "He sang like a cherub. I am sure they'll find him a spot in the play." Once the impressive production of *California Gold* was completed ten weeks later, I thanked the director profusely for including Reid. "He brought so much positive energy to the stage," was her summary. I had to agree.

---

Music was creatively embedded into Reid's school day at several schools he attended which also helped him generalize valuable skills. At one, the principal played guitar and greeted Reid after his long bus ride with a transitional song to begin his day. This created a predictable routine and front-loaded the expectation of a great day. The same school turned a music room into Reid's "office" to inspire him to do his best work there, and encouraged iPod breaks. Together with classmates, he wrote a jingle for the school's vending machine business. They also recorded a song as a fund-raiser for the school. Their talent show was better than the Grammys, in my opinion.

In contrast, the rigid behavioral school Reid attended provides an example of what not to do. They had a music room, but students had to earn the privilege of using it as a reward for completed work. It was often withheld from Reid, which was problematic and demotivating. For a child with a strong affinity for music, their policy was akin to making him earn oxygen or a healthy breakfast.

They had effectively removed his lifeline and reason for trying. Music can be used to motivate, but when it was removed as a consequence, it set off a mutiny in Reid's case. They used his desire for music to manipulate rather than teach. This same school prohibited students from going out in the community if they had any maladaptive behaviors. They had to earn that right also. How in the world can you practice desired skills in a vacuum, without seeing typical peers and behaviors as a model to mimic?

When Reid attended a highly competitive, distinguished public high school with more than 2,500 students, he wanted to enter their "Idol" singing contest. Generalizing his skill to yet another setting with many new people, he performed "Shine," his debut original, for the first time without Angela, the band, or me present. This was a huge milestone that came after significant consternation and anxiety. He wavered all morning in anguished self-talk.

His aide texted me status updates. "He says he's too nervous."

I texted back, "That's common; don't offer any rewards or appear to make him do it. Just let him talk it through himself. He usually decides to do it in the eleventh hour, as long as it's his own choice." Only I wasn't sure this time, without any of his usual entourage. I had to let it go. "Tell him it's up to him."

Then at last, what I wanted to read from around the corner where I was parked: "He's gonna do it. He's going on."

At the last minute, from a concrete slab amphitheater in the center of the grassy quad, Reid announced to the gathered student body that he would sing "Shine" a cappella. That was a first! The song itself became the constant amid numerous other variables, including the spotty sound system.

In essence, he was introducing himself at this new school, telling his story to a group of typical teens at lunchtime through the lyrics. Quite possibly, his performance inspired some of them in the process. He and Angela had done what composer Eric Whitacre suggests, "Write the music your inside-you needs your outside-you to hear."

*Some days I feel grand*
*With the sun on my face and my feet in the sand*
*I can do anything*
*Whatever the day may bring*

*The clouds roll in and the sky turns gray*
*I can't find the words to say*
*I don't know what to do*
*I see some light is breaking through*

*You can do it if you really try*
*Don't give up, reach for the sky*
*A spark in you has begun to grow*
*Shout it for the world to know, you're gonna*
*Shine......Shine......Shine*

*Sing with your heart*
*Play your part*
*Jump to your feet*
*Dance in the street*
*Don't be afraid*
*Let others see*
*The dreams you have*
*What you could be*

I received a picture of him post-performance, adrenaline rushing, arm in arm, flanked by his vocal coach, Frank, and the school band director, who was one of the judges. It wasn't about winning that day, but rather being included, mastering independence, and generalizing his musicianship to a new crowd and venue. Throngs of students stood to applaud, surely never imagining that the conspicuous boy they passed in the halls with his own instructional aide was capable of this.

If you've watched enough bonus material on two-disc collector's edition versions of Disney films, you have heard composer Richard Sherman explain that Walt wanted the music to move the plot forward. He says, "A successful song for a musical, on the stage or screen, is not just pleasant listening. It tells a story, conveys character and personality. It's the most difficult thing to do. You're writing the whole book on the head of a pin." The songs that Angela helped Reid compose were certainly moving the plotline of his life forward.

Angela consulted with the band teacher afterward to strategize ways Reid could participate more fully in her orchestra class. His special interest opened a door to considering more inclusion with typical peers. Although he did not play an instrument at the same level as the other students, he could pass out music, play percussion, help tune the strings at the keyboard, or count them off.

—♪—

Vacation, as well as school, can be an opportune time to generalize skills. We travel to my mom's house on Nantucket for an annual summer sojourn. Why not get an out-of-town gig? I fished around for the right venue and discovered a new pop-up pocket park concert series on Saturday mornings. We found a guitarist available to accompany Reid, creating another opportunity to generalize skills in Reid's area of special interest as they rehearsed and performed.

He was going to make music in a new place, which made it a success already. Turns out the press on Nantucket covered the concert and wrote a story about Reid. Being interviewed afterward was yet another way to generalize conversation skills. The reporter wrote, "At the conclusion of each song, those assembled would applaud, only to be drowned out by Reid returning the favor, calling out, 'Thank you! You're awesome!' To those walking by...one thing was certainly clear: this young man enjoyed what he was doing."

Generalizing skills to new settings will happen first and most smoothly in the area of your child's special interest. Look for ways to share their acumen with new groups. If they are passionate about trains, could they display their collection at your bunko group? If their fixation is on dinosaurs, maybe a local museum is a good place to write spelling words or generalize a skill. An after-school club or library can be a novel place to practice social skills. Let your child experience being uncomfortable and then feeling pride by taking a skill they've accomplished to new people. The mastery and confidence that result will raise the bar on what is possible back in the familiar setting as well as in any number of other new places. You never know where an affinity will take you.

*What is a natural next step for your child?*

*Name an impossible goal for your child that might just be possible?*

*Can you think of a new environment where your child can practice a familiar skill?*

# 12

*Ensemble Playing*

Included in Life

## Ensemble Playing

*The beauty of playing in different ensembles—concert bands, marching bands, symphony orchestras, jazz ensembles, pit orchestras—is not only the exposure to different repertoire but also developing an understanding of how one's instrument and part fit into the whole. It requires generosity, since there is no place for ego in an ensemble; one must set aside their own personality and defer to others. Ensembles offer a place where students can find a niche, a place to excel and feel good about their music. The interaction, mixing of ideas, the give and take, and community make it deeply rewarding.*

*The ultimate ensemble for our children might be what educators call inclusion. We want our children with special needs to interact with typical peers for as long as possible, since that is where they will mimic the highest level of functioning and have the least restrictive environment. Their presence creates potential for their classmates as well. "Inclusion elevates all," as Elaine Hall, founder of the Miracle Project, has wisely observed.*

# 12

## Included in Life

*The aim of God in history is the creation of an all-inclu-
sive community of loving persons, with Himself included
in that community as its prime sustainer and most glorious
inhabitant.*

—DALLAS WILLARD, AMERICAN PHILOSOPHER

Inclusion was a long time coming for us. Of course, at this point
in the book, you can guess, it came through music. I pushed the
powers that be for full inclusion from the time Reid was in kindergarten. His behaviors and needs were so great that teacher after
teacher after administrator couldn't find a way to offer it for very
much of the day. It came in snatches, though, at church, in drama
programs, and when he entered the large public high school.

When Reid was seventeen, I wanted to expand his influences,
notably with other male music teachers. His voice was changing
and it seemed opportune to have him emulate more tenor and
baritone voices. We found several young worship leaders—Manny,
Brendan, and Frank—who enjoyed Reid's enthusiasm and were
able to teach him without specialized autism training as long as

they stuck to music. I enrolled him in a typical music studio that had a different "look and feel" than the music therapy clinic Angela had opened. He went from being the verbal, high-functioning one to being the only one with an obvious disability. Now he would rub shoulders with typical peers, albeit mostly younger, in the waiting room and at recitals. Raising the bar, like playing tennis with the club pro, is always an opportunity for improvement.

At his first recital with the new studio, he sang "This Is What I Believe," a song he and Angela wrote as his statement of faith when he was baptized at the beach. This time, Frank accompanied him on piano instead of Angela on guitar. He introduced himself Kingsmen-style. "Hello, I'm Reid." (*Little wave.*) "This is Frank. Hi, Frank." (*Little wave.*) "Are ya' ready, Frank?" It may have puzzled the audience, but no one got up and left. In fact, by the end, two ladies in the front, who apparently shared our faith, stood and clapped vigorously.

At the second recital six months later, he watched with interest as another teenage boy and girl did a duet of a popular song from the radio. On the way home, he announced, "Mom, I have a brilliant idea. I want to do a duet. Who could do it with me?" The lightbulbs in our heads flashed at the same time.

"Juliana!" we echoed in unison.

Juliana was another vocal student as well as the studio assistant who greeted us each week at the reception desk. The next Tuesday, Reid marched in on a mission. "Juliana, can we do a duet together?"

With a great big smile, she said, "Yes!"

They spent the next six months rehearsing Of Monsters and Men's hit, "Little Talks." Another marker, inclusion was set to music that night with its own magic and mutual benefit. As Paula Kluth has said, "Special education is not a place." It was an experience Reid and Juliana will never forget.

*Hey! Hey! Hey!*
*I don't like walking around this old and empty house*
*So hold my hand, I'll walk with you, my dear*
*The stairs creak as you sleep, it's keeping me awake*
*It's the house telling you to close your eyes*

*And some days I can't even dress myself*
*It's killing me to see you this way*

*'Cause though the truth may vary*
*This ship will carry our bodies safe to shore*

Our children learn so much by watching others. It can be very em-powering and advantageous to observe and interact with typical peers in their area of expertise. Ultimately though, it is the typical partners who learn the most from inclusion. Maya Angelou says, "It is time for parents to teach young people early on that in diversity there is beauty and there is strength." By interacting with students with special needs, typical students learn patience, gratitude, com-passion, kindness, creativity, and humility. It can literally change their lives. I am aware of at least five high school seniors who have writ-ten their college admission essays about interacting with Reid. Some were in that preschool circle time; others met him at baseball or through music. One has gone on to study speech therapy, two will be music therapists, another is in corporate real estate, and yet another is studying public relations. Hearing about the positive impact he has had on others redeems the challenges we have faced. His difficulties and struggles have served a higher purpose in shaping responsible, compassionate leaders in the world. It is hard to explain how gratify-ing it was to receive this email out of the blue recently:

*I stumbled across Reid's website by searching for the music therapy Jam Sessions on Google. I just began my Master of Arts in Teaching and Dual Credential in English and Special Education program at Point Loma Nazarene University, which I am very excited about.*

*One of the original reasons I became interested in special education was because I worked with a young boy about 10 years ago who was named Reid at a Christian Youth Theatre program at Santa Fe Christian School. He and I worked together over the course of the program's classes and it was such a joy to watch him perform with his classmates at the end of the program. What I am wondering is: Could this be the same Reid?*

It was indeed. They had both benefitted from that brief encounter created because a theater group was willing to make accommodations to include all students in their after-school program.

For us, full inclusion is a myth. What we have experienced is more as Torrie Dunlap of Kids Included Together[19] describes it. "I believe that 'special' has become a euphemism for 'separate.' When we create separate places for children where their 'special needs' can be met, we are teaching them that their place is over there, with people like them and not in the full community." What Reid did enjoy was more like partial inclusion. It came in fits and starts that were short and sweet, then could be extended. Dunlap continues, "Full inclusion" sounds very prescribed. I much prefer meaningful, authentic and intentional inclusion. Letting it come organically from a young person's interests, strengths and talents is the way to go." Inclusion is worth inching toward incrementally because it

---

19 Kids Included Together (KIT) teaches inclusive practices to people and organizations that serve children and youth. KITonline.org

mutually benefits our children and the typical ones who gain just as much, if not more. Look for ways and places your child can be included, especially in their areas of special interest. It will expand their perception of themselves and your hope for what is possible.

*What can your child do with typical peers?*

*Where does your child fit in or belong?*

*Who could benefit by helping to include your child (at church, in your neighborhood, or school)?*

# 13

*Improvisation*

Never Mind the Box

## Improvisation

*To improvise is to compose, perform, or deliver on the spur of the moment, without preparation. Musical improvisation is the creative activity of composing in the moment. Improv combines performance with communication of emotions, instrumental technique, and spontaneous response to other musicians. Improv sets one free from being right and wrong because you can make it up as you go along. It requires mental agility, reading inferences, thinking on your feet, risk taking, and flexibility.*

*Parenting children who learn differently requires improvisation from the get-go and designing relevant adult vocation for them all the more so. Combining what we know about their special interests with the freedom to think creatively and abandon preconceived notions can yield exciting results.*

# 13

## Never Mind the Box

*It's kind of fun to do the impossible.*

—WALT DISNEY

Thinking outside the box is not enough for our kids who are differently abled. We need to really believe, and behave as if, there are no boxes. We need to look for ways to remove the boxes that confine them and instead build figurative ramps that bring them out of the corners into center stage.

When Reid completed high school, the logical progression was for him to move to the adult-transition program in our school district and begin workability vocational services. This would involve learning to ride public transportation and folding pizza boxes for short periods of the day with assistance. While those are valuable skills and practice, we knew he would need something more to satisfy his creative passion and stay motivated.

My husband and I brainstormed possibilities on a dinner date. Some permutation of radio work was an option; it might be more sustainable than the music as a weekday gig. Maybe he could recite public service announcements (PSAs) with some on-air personalities we knew. I had read about a radio station featuring adults with disabilities on Staten Island. "Anything with a microphone," I wondered out loud. "What if he interviewed people in the autism community—his teachers and therapists?"

Jim is a consummate marketing genius and doesn't mince words. "Who wants to listen to that?" Did I mention his Command, Achiever, Strategic, Futuristic strengths? He did build on my suggestion, though. "What if he had his own special-interest talk show—like Ali G. or Charlie Rose—with guests that people really want to hear? It might be interesting content to put a kid with autism in the driver's seat. We could pop them up on SoundCloud and see what happens."

He had me. "That's it!"

At the very least, Reid would be interested in doing it. That was the main point anyway: to give him a productive, motivating aim in life, in lieu of leaving for college or choosing a degree. Jim was more than supportive; he was excited and fully vested. That alone gave me the confidence to pursue it. He was partnering in new ways, right at the time I was losing my relevance to a nearly adult male son. Besides, it wouldn't cost us anything to try.

On the way home from the wine-shop bistro, we named it *Talk Time* after one of our family bedside rituals. When Reid was little, our best bet for connecting was to create a routine time and place for conversation. At dinner, we each shared a high point and low point of the day. But, bedtime worked the best especially if it happened like clockwork. Talk Time meant tête-à-tête; it was the time when heads had hit pillows and we could get eye to eye to review the day, anticipate tomorrow, and say prayers. That's when our best connection time happened. No one loved branding more than Reid.

As he was turning twenty, mostly as an experiment, we posted the first *Talk Time with Reid Moriarty*, a biweekly podcast where

Reid interviews people he finds interesting, and you might, too. Beginning with a few willing neighbors and familiar clerks in the neighborhood, in short order, we reached out to the CEO of the Rock and Roll Hall of Fame in our hometown of Cleveland, Ohio. I've memorized his pithy reply to Jim's cold-call e-mail. "Absolutely! Karen will schedule it." He won my heart. Encouraged by the favorable response, we kept going. People were amazingly supportive when we made an easy and specific way for them to participate. Samuel Adams, a character actor at the Boston Tea Party Museum, said yes, then so did one of the Rockettes. We were on our way.

*Talk Time* was giving us a great family project if nothing else. Jim designed the logo, tapped into his network to invite guests, and masterminded the brand. I edited the audio in GarageBand, prepped the questions with Reid, and supervised the details. It gave us a focus when he was out of school—which I sometimes dreaded—and when we traveled. Suddenly, for the first time, he was hooked into the destination and itinerary whether we were going to Cleveland, New York City, or Vancouver. Researching each guest gave him age-appropriate alternatives and reasons to be online. Posing for pictures and writing thank-you notes afterward were social skills embedded in the process, not to mention the language processing and conversation skills required for the interview itself.

Perhaps the most prominent interview to date has been with the head writer of Sesame Street and his puppet alter ego, Murray Monster. Sesame Street has an initiative with Autism Speaks to "See Amazing in All Children." Joey Mazzarino did just that with Reid. His interview was an out-of-body experience for us. A place that was the pinnacle of creativity and imagination was welcoming Reid. Their children's programming consumed so much of his childhood and free time even as an adolescent. Now he could interact with its creators and announce his special interest with unabashed joy and have it reciprocated. I had not seen Reid's enthusiasm matched by an adult, until we watched Joey Mazzarino outdo him in energy, zeal, and quick thinking as if he were a clean, educational, and kind stand-up comic.

Reid keeps a mental wish list of people he wants to interview. Ellen DeGeneres is on it, Ryan Seacrest, and a bunch of Nashvillians, if we ever make it there. I have learned from my friend, Sandi, to honor his dreams. Her son, Joel, had wanted to go to China from a very young age. Rather than laugh at his lofty pipe dream or tell him it was out of the question, she tucked it away and let him dabble in a little Mandarin. Recently, at twenty-two, he fulfilled that dream and went to Jiaozuo, China, with a mission team of educators and therapists. He painted murals on the walls of an orphanage for special needs children. His aspirations weren't necessarily his mom's, but she took them seriously and helped him achieve them. Can you imagine how his very presence as a young adult on the spectrum encouraged and expanded the Chinese staff's sense of what is possible for the special needs orphans in their charge?

I have learned to correct myself every time I am tempted to diminish or undermine Reid's ambition. I hear some of you thinking, "Yeah, right. That's great for you, but my kid will never have a podcast or go to China." I know; that's exactly the point. Your child has their *own* strength and special interest. What does she dream of doing? What would be the perfect niche for him? We have a friend with Down syndrome who grew up sewing and helping her mother at their Sew Inspired stitch lounge and sewing school. At nineteen, the daughter just launched her own new business, Jasmine's Bunting Co. Jasmine employs five peers who are jazzed to have such a relevant and social alternative to their adult day program. Not unlike an old-fashioned sewing circle, they work together to fulfill custom orders and create an inventory of hand-sewn celebration flags to sell. They promise every bunting flag is sewn with love and I can attest that they turn any room, mantel, or mirror into a party.

We know another young adult on the spectrum who paints abstract impressionistic images that represent various people in his life. His family has helped him set up an art studio where he spends the day painting and interacting with other visual artists. They are exhibiting his work in corporate offices. Another student might dream of living independently or driving a car. I know young men who have done both recently, against all odds. "Impossible things are happening every…day," to quote Rodgers & Hammerstein from *Cinderella*.

I love the great experiment that Jia Jiang, author of *Rejection Proof*, embarked upon. He made absurd requests of total strangers for one hundred days in order to desensitize himself to rejection. He figured hearing "no" over and over would help him break through his fear. The surprise came when everyone he asked said "yes." A policeman let him drive his squad car, a clerk made Olympic rings out of doughnuts, and a stranger let him borrow one hundred dollars. He did indeed bust his fears and built the confidence to help others do the same. I think of him every time I e-mail a celebrity to ask for an interview.

Many times in life, the process matters more than the product. Embracing the misfires and comedy that ensue with each *Talk Time* interview, we landed on a format that presents Reid at his best and scaffolds both parties in a positive encounter. Intuitively, after years of studying Reid, maximizing his strengths, looking for mentors, and defining success in small steps, we had apparently incorporated the elements required to keep Reid motivated and learning into adulthood. The accidental genius of it became more and more obvious.

For starters, it's a series. I've often said, "We never do anything once." As for many kids with ASD, the third time is the charm for Reid. We don't even evaluate a new activity until after he does it several times. The first and second time only count for learning the mechanics and knowing what to expect. Each episode of *Talk Time* has an intro and outro; the newness is sandwiched into a familiar template. The consistency means Reid knows what to expect, yet he can be spontaneous within that, and of course, each guest is a variation on the structured theme. It's the perfect blend of predictability and novelty. Reid's interview questions vary with each guest, but several standbys are repeated each time as comforting buoys. Each conversation is short and sweet; we keep our promise to take just twenty minutes of the interviewees' time. Of course, Reid chooses the guests so every encounter is highly preferred and he's in charge of the conversation. Like a chart hit with a sticky chorus, Reid couldn't get *Talk Time* off his mind.

What we didn't expect was how much Reid would enjoy listening to the final product himself. He pours over them on the SoundCloud app on my phone as if they were movie trailers. Like ultrapersonalized social stories[20] or *Model Me* teaching videos, they train him for future conversations on and off the record. Through the repetition, he is able to memorize idioms, expressions, pauses, volume of laughter, as well as the actual life lessons and advice reiterated from people he admires most. His review reinforces skill development and improvement through self-correction with participants who willingly overlook his mistakes while modeling

---

20 Social stories are valuable tools devised by Carol Gray in 1991, as tools to help individuals on the autism spectrum better understand the nuances of interpersonal communication.

natural interaction. Their interest in him is undeniably powerful, creating an intense emotional context, however brief.

I hear him quoting snatches of interviews verbatim. "That's what Babbie Mason says, 'I let the applause go through me, up to God.'" He has expanded his vocabulary by copying Irish lead singer, Chris Llewellyn, with a choice adjective, "Brilliant!" By reviewing the concentrated, edited versions of high-interest conversations, he also seems to have improved his pragmatic skills of waiting to interrupt and clarifying with follow-up questions. In a sense, Reid has taken his ongoing speech therapy on the road with celebrities rather than speech therapists, and generalized it outside the clinic and classroom. His lifelong language goals are being accomplished with people of his own choosing.

*Talk Time* often turns out to be hysterically funny. Each podcast gives listeners a glimpse into the personalities of people they wouldn't otherwise get to meet and a window into how Reid's mind works. Somewhat stealthily, we are spreading autism awareness. Without ever using the label, Reid educates and illustrates how the disability impacts him, yet doesn't impede his ability to find common ground and a way to connect. Isak Dinesen, author of *Out of Africa*, wrote, "To be a person is to have a story to tell."

*Talk Time* celebrates the personhood of the special guest and the unlikely talk show host. Through the dialogue, each is showing the other how to relate, how to care, even how to love another human being, whether they are famous, make sense all the time, take an interest in you, or just crossed your path that day. It was Dave Isay of Storycorps who said, "Listening is an act of love." It turns out you don't have to know all the answers or all the questions, to show kindness. Surely after fifteen minutes with Reid, each guest knows a bit more about autism and learns that it can be accompanied with great joy. Each of them is learning to love.

I love the irony of a talk show whose host has a "lifelong disability that impacts social, language, and behavior skills."[21] A young man who might otherwise be marginalized is given full access and invited into the limelight to engage with prominent figures in green rooms where others are prohibited from entering. George Saunders notes, "Irony is just honesty with the volume cranked up." Not that we planned all that. Remember, we were just looking for something more relevant than folding pizza boxes. It was the culmination of these fifteen principles applied over time, that resulted in a niche pursuit for Reid.

We have released a one-year anniversary video of behind-the-scenes snippets and audio bloopers that Reid has let slip during interviews. What we don't capture on tape is the resistance and anxiety that sometimes precedes the interviews especially when we are in a new place. Five minutes before our scheduled time to grill the Boston Red Sox organist, Reid was unsure about entering Fenway Park. We had passed through the barkers and beer vendors on Yawkey Way so he had a preview, but it involved a lot of what irks him: throngs of jostling people, loud noises, and mixed institutional food smells. Thankful for the pregame passes that granted us entrance at a press gate, we proceeded with caution to a cordoned area. Calmly, our crew—Allie, Jim, Reid and I—sat in the distinctive green stadium seats, waiting for our contact person. As she approached, Reid let out his classic acquiescence, "All right, I will interview Josh Kantor." We bank on established patterns. And he nails it every time. Did we stay for the rousing game and see the stadium full to capacity? What do you think?

It dawns on me afresh that through *Talk Time*, Reid is actually listening to other people's stories. Larry King had some experience

---

21 The classic definition of autism

with this and noted, "I remind myself every morning: Nothing I say this day will teach me anything. So if I'm going to learn, I must do it by listening." Whether it is Ralph Rubio, owner of the Mexican food chain, explaining his first job, or Keb' Mo,' the blues singer, giving songwriting tips, Reid is learning by listening. This is how he has always learned: through music and story, the whole brain, gestalt way. Story and song are truly intertwined as the Songstream Project motto claims.

*Talk Time* feels like the sum of all the parts in Reid's life. We never imagined it; we just kept putting one step in front of the other, trying to stay ahead of him with something productive. It is only in hindsight that we see how the steps connected in a grand plan. Reid still falters in an unplanned conversation on the fly, even with a familiar person, but the structure of *Talk Time* enables him to experience success. I hope this Never-Mind-the-Box concept will help you imagine something totally unique that suits your child's special interest and strengths. What would it look like at your house to remove the box, connect with the world, and let your child's affinity lead the way?

*What is the ideal job description for your child as an adult?*

*If the sky was the limit (i.e. money, behavior, timing was no object) what could you see your child doing?*

*What box needs to be removed for your child to blossom?*

# 14

*Choosing Repertoire*

Define Success

## Choosing Repertoire

*Repertoire refers to the pieces of music a musician has learned and can perform. More than just choosing pieces to play, selecting repertoire defines a curriculum and a set of beliefs. These choices require commitment, exposure, and risk: commitment because the music we play defines our values, exposure because we share this repertoire with an audience, and risk because what we select may not always resonate with others.*

*In the course of life, we all make decisions that define us. What we believe, what we value, and how we define success make up a repertoire for each of us as individuals and as a family. These free-will choices may not always resonate with those around us, but they become our legacy.*

# 14

## Define Success

*No good fish goes anywhere without a porpoise.*

—LEWIS CARROLL, AUTHOR OF *ALICE'S ADVENTURES IN WONDERLAND*

Defining success in parenting, marriage, personal life, or career is crucial to knowing where you are going and when you have arrived. Rather than thinking of success as some looming or elusive aspiration, I've learned to break it into smaller definitive steps that can be mastered and measured. Defining both the steps and the end point keeps us from getting discouraged when success for us looks different than it does for others. In some ways, this principle actually becomes *redefining* success in the face of cultural norms and expectations.

I've learned this principle from Jim. He hammers it home as soon as he arrives from work as a stock response to almost every question I run by him. "What if we go to Hawaii after Christmas?" "Do you think so-and-so would be on the Banding Together board?" "Should we get a table for Reid at the Chalk Festival in Covina?" "What do you think of this new rug for the kitchen?"

No matter what the topic, his answer is usually another question, "What does success look like?"

What he means is, "Spell out for me what you really want to accomplish. Then, and only then will I be able to determine my answer."

I am surprised how I stutter, hem, and haw in reply. I want to say, "That's not what I asked you! Don't change the subject with another question. Just tell me if you like this rug." However, I've come to value the process. Actually articulating what success would look like puts me one step closer to knowing what to do. As I answer him, sometimes the plan changes entirely. Other times, it becomes obvious how to modify, adapt, or abandon the idea for something better and more targeted to really meet the need. In the rug example, defining success forces me to realize whether I am after warm feet in the morning or an enhanced visual aesthetic. Slippers might be a better solution in the case of the former, a candle in the latter. Knowing what success looks like can change everything.

It reminds me of Reid's occupational therapist, Brenda, when he was just four. Given his seemingly insurmountable sensory needs, she orchestrated some very messy and wacky activities with blurred boundaries, at least to my mom's 1950s way of thinking. Drawing with shaving cream and peanut butter on a mat with toddlers in the family room just violated her sense of decency. Sounding a bit like Mr. Banks when he came home to a houseful of chimney sweeps, she questioned the therapist on her reasoning. "What is the meaning of this? Shouldn't we be teaching him to keep food at the table and wash his hands?"

Brenda calmly explained, "Well, it depends what goal we are working on." Basically, she was not teaching manners at that particular time. She was targeting interaction with peers and fine motor muscle development. In that session, success looked like eye contact with the play partners, and Reid using both his pointer fingers. Defining success enabled her to deal with the clean up afterward and see the point of the whole, sticky process. She was masterful at isolating goals and chipping away at them in creative and playful ways.

Now that Reid is older, defining goals one at a time might mean that we work on a firm handshake during an interview and leave eye contact alone, or prioritize singing into the microphone rather than holding still at a gig. Other times, a teachable moment about character presents itself and supersedes whatever we set out to do. Narrowing down the number of videos to buy at a thrift store might be a lesson on functional math or discernment, depending on the day.

I have started to use this principle back on Jim. With a box of five hundred *Purple Party* CDs to sell, I proposed we set up a display in our driveway during the annual neighborhood garage sale. Not a fan of garage sales at all, Jim heckled me and thought the whole idea was ridiculous. "We won't sell any; it's not the right crowd. Why are you wasting your time?"

Having learned his language and internalized this principle, I had the foresight the night before to say, "You want to know what success looks like tomorrow? Success is engaging with our neighbors." I was off the hook. Now it didn't matter how few CDs we sold; the effort would be worth it as long as I got to interact with a handful of neighbors we rarely see and update them on Reid's endeavors. Jim still taunted me as he and Reid drove off for a hike, but at least the expectations were clear.

Defining success is more than merely managing expectations, damage control, or making the best of a bad situation. It is about optimizing outcomes, opportunities and performance.

When we know what success looks like in advance, we can focus our attention on that priority, break big goals into achiev-
able smaller steps, be more attune to specific modifications that
might be helpful, and recruit the help needed. What's more, we
know when we are done and can be specific about celebrating
accomplishments. Defining success determines the how and
why of what we do and helps us to be satisfied with the results
and stay motivated.

~♭~

It was quite a coup when Reid got a *Talk Time* interview with
Temple Grandin. Jim happened to be out of town so Allie, Reid,
and I had to navigate downtown Los Angeles by ourselves and
planned to spend the night in a hotel. Temple was in town for a
large benefit event. We bought the expensive tickets and did our
best to prepare for the sensory overload that defines downtown
LA making it a landmine for Reid. Success was defined as getting the ten-minute interview, not necessarily staying for the concert, hearing her speak, networking with the other guests, seeing
American Idol contestant James Durbin live, or having breakfast
with anyone the next morning.

Tension mounted with the variables of the unfamiliar urban
environment. Allie and I exchanged an apprehensive eye roll at
several points as we encountered the forced valet parking, long
line at check in, and broom closet of a bathroom. The smoky hotel
lobby and crowded pool didn't do much to pacify any of us. If I
was anxious, I knew Reid was just barely holding it together. He
clutched my arm on the up escalator as we found the unmarked
entrance. We were outside the box and our comfort zone. Inside
the darkened Club Nokia, the organizers had their own pre-event

jitters. Our contact was buzzing and sending mixed messages of where we should stand or wait.

"Temple's coming." Everyone was nervous about her being in the house. It would have been much simpler had we done the interview in the hotel lobby where we had passed her sitting waiting seconds earlier. I knew Reid would snap into gear and accomplish his mission once we got out of the swirling mayhem; it is just the blasted before and after that threaten to unravel him. I know what Gustav Mahler means when he says, "The real art of conducting consists in transitions."

As predicted, Reid did the interview with characteristic aplomb, and we left through the nearest marked exit. The grandiose original plan had been to take a swim, then return for the actual event. Allie and I were giddy with relief as we watched Reid dance his sillies out under the Grammy Museum marquis to a Taylor Swift song they piped onto the sidewalk. Even when I bought the tickets, I wasn't sure whether Reid would sit through the event itself. Had Jim been with us, we would have had the flexibility to tag team, one of us leave with Reid and two others stay. But without him, I couldn't resist pulling the plug. "Who votes we drive home right now?" It was unanimous, so we did. We had carefully defined success and could let go of the rest.

In my younger days, I would have pushed to have it all and satisfy my Achiever strength. Did you want to know my top five strengths now? Empathy, Harmony, Achiever, Responsibility, and Significance. But I am older and wiser now, and have learned to work with others. Success was getting the interview. We had that, so we could leave smiling, holding our heads high with no disappointments. Less is more, in songwriting and in life.

Defining success is effective for individual events as well as the course of a school year or an entire life. Our pastor, Mark Foreman, talks about defining ultimate success in parenting. When asked, parents almost by default say their goal is that their kids be happy. Success in parenting needs to be more than that, or we are all in trouble when those kids are set loose in the world at twenty-one. Success has to be more than happiness or we will have failed both our children and society. For Mark and his wife, Jan, the definition came down to having kids who loved God and loved others well. By that plumb line, they could measure and evaluate all their decisions. Defining success in the big picture makes day-to-day decisions clearer.

Admittedly, for us at times, success meant keeping our marriage intact or our family together, under one roof. At other times, in the day-to-day reality, success is staying off the television or trying a new food. A successful airline flight might be one with forgiving seatmates or without incident; it has nothing to do with finishing a book, having time to eat, or a smooth landing. You get the idea. When success is clearly defined, we can major on the majors. I think each family can define success in both the wide lens and the zoom. It will morph over time, but don't cheat and change it midstream. Having a singular definitive statement of what success looks like gives us certainty of a job well done and a reason to celebrate afterward. Like a notification pinging on your smartphone, defining success allows for feedback on the status of a singular goal rather than aimless living and uncertainty of progress. Sometimes our kids' milestones seem invisible or infinitesimal to the rest of the world so it is up to us to define them, call them out, chip away at them, anchor them, and be encouraged to continue.

For our children on the spectrum—challenged as they are— one overarching way to define success is that they would be able to connect in relationships, to give and receive love. This naturally becomes our focus because it is precisely what they do differently from the norm. We weren't as intentional as the Foremans, but I can see how by any definition, success for us was fueled by music. Rock and blues pioneer Edgar Winter knows, "Music is very spiritual, it has the power to bring people together." It has certainly brought and kept our family together. We have had countless crazy dance parties in the kitchen, played deejay in the car on long and short road trips, and used it to transition off the all-consuming electronic screen time. Both our dogs, Benny and Norah, had theme songs (Elton John's "Bennie and the Jets" and Norah Jones's "Feeling the Same Way"). Music is the common ground for relating when Reid asks his *Talk Time* guests, "What's at the top of your playlist?" Of course, he brings up *Mary Poppins* on almost every podcast as well, and she made it into the "Purple Party" song lyrics.

In tangible, concrete, and audible ways, music has enabled Reid to relate to God as well as to others, which is perhaps the most profound thing about it. There's an expression in surfing attributed to Phil Edwards that "the best surfer is the one having the most fun." Could this also be true on stage and in all of life? For the release party of Reid's *Purple Party* CD, we rented an ice cream truck; well, actually, it was a customized, souped-up, ice cream Harley motorcycle. It pulled into the grassy, park-like setting with music jangling at the set break. I prepaid for sixty treats so the kids and adults could pick what they wanted from Isaac, the leather-clad ice cream man. Black is the new white for the Good Humor Man, I guess. In booking this festive addition to the party, they asked what message we'd like written on the menu board that was mounted on the motorcycle. I toyed with "All free today," a line from *Chitty Chitty Bang Bang* that we quote freely around the house when any sugar is involved. Then I remembered it was the child catcher who says that, and it didn't seem fair to put Isaac in a bad light. I texted Jim, and he had a great idea. Riffing off the lyrics of the "Purple Party" chorus, he suggested, "Price of Ice Cream = One Purple Dance." Thus it read.

*We're gonna dance all night at our purple party*
*Put your polka dot shoes on*
*We're gonna dance all night at our purple party*
*Put your party hats on*

*Show us your purple dance*
*Show us your purple dance*
*Show us your purple dance*

It was Pastor Mark who was most smitten by the text. He took photos of it and helped us see it as a picture of the gospel. Jesus paid the price for all us. All we have to do for our part is accept the free gift, live life to the fullest, and do the dance! Neither hard work nor good works have any bearing on the gift. People lined up for the ice cream, of course, but some struggled visibly with the cost. They'd have rather paid cash or worked to earn their Dove bar than risk embarrassment. The chance of looking silly by wiggling their hips or raising their arms paralyzed them in fear. *Free? Dance? Um…but I can't. I won't.* The free gift didn't compute, nor did the unabashed joy of dancing.

That much Reid gets. He can "show you his purple dance" any time of the day or night with total abandon. His lack of pride, self-consciousness, and regard for social pressure is an enviable freedom. It makes him both open to the gospel and a walking example of it. In this sense, his inability becomes a gift and his lack of inhibition an example to follow. As a kinesthetic learner myself, Reid is just the three-dimensional reminder I need of spiritual truths that I say I believe, but often forget or just rattle off by rote. Having them acted them out on a daily basis plants them permanently into my flesh and blood. He is blessed to be a blessing.

Music is spiritual in nature; the fact that we understand rhythm in the womb and are born with it indicates to me that it reflects God's image in which we are made. The Westminster Shorter Catechism defines "the chief end of man is to glorify God, and to enjoy him forever." That sounds like worship to me. While worship can be done silently or bodily, most often, it is accompanied by music. It was St. Augustine who said, "He who sings prays twice." Music somehow transports us into another realm. In that worshipful realm we experience who we are in relationship to God. We comprehend who He is and what we are not. We grasp the fullness of being created in his image, made for relationship, able to think, feel, and express.

For me, music is the language of the spirit. No matter how disabled a child's body or mind might be, I believe their spirit is intact. Music puts us in touch with that part of them that is whole and well. Vice versa, music puts that part of them in touch with God and us. It connects us at a deeper level than words ever will. Jon Foreman of Switchfoot says it this way, "Music for me has been more than just an individual pursuit; it's been a vehicle, a way to examine the world, and a planet unto itself that I can go to and look back at our own planet with fresh eyes. I feel like music, in many ways, is a scaffolding for the soul that allows you to reach new places you can't go without it."

Truth be told, we are all broken people in a broken world. Music transports us to a higher place where we will be whole. Singing in worship to our God is a declaration that fuels our hope in a reality yet to come where we will literally join with angels in the continual music that Revelation 5 describes as rushing waters. Making music is one of the ways God's kingdom comes on earth as it is in heaven. In the meantime, God "inhabits the praises of his people" according to Psalm 22, which definitely motivates me to sing.

⸎

Indulge me in one last movie reference? We all make mistakes along the way. Even sweet little Charlie Bucket messed up and stole fizzy lifting drinks from Willy Wonka's chocolate factory. But, if we maintain our allegiance to God, in the end, He invites us to reign with Him over His entire kingdom, not just a chocolate factory. That's the promise of Revelation 20:6 and 2 Timothy 2:12: "If we endure, we will also reign with Him." When convicted of his misstep, Charlie was contrite, and also clear that the Everlasting Gobstopper belonged to Mr. Wonka. He relinquished it in a winning display of loyalty, despite Grandpa Joe's vote to give it to Slugworth in revenge. Wonka was ecstatic. "You won! You did it! You did it! I knew you would! Oh Charlie..."

God is a good, good God who allows tests and trials in our lives. He roots for us like his home team and wants to help us succeed. He loves us sacrificially and created us to spend time with Him. The Creator wants to include everybody.

All of us have a laundry list of fifty-two things that could go wrong in a day whether it's a remote getting thrown, a check bouncing, or a rained out event. I can think of another fifty-two ways to improve Reid's program and I ruminate over a few burning unanswerable questions—like how to prevent teeth grinding and where Reid will live as an adult—instead of counting sheep at night. In response, I keep keenly aware that God is sovereign, and nothing happens that He has not allowed in our lives because He can turn it into good. So when the shoe drops, or the dog barks, or Reid does the unexpected, it doesn't rattle me like it used to. There is music to look forward to, on heaven and on earth. And that eclipses the negativity and imperfection.

Whatever God's plan is for me (and my family), I am going to have a good attitude about it and do it for His glory. In Psalm 16, David, who some argue was the first music therapist playing for sheep as well as the king, has a beautiful way of embracing God's purpose and defining success:

> *Lord, you alone are my portion and my cup;*
> *you make my lot secure.*

> *The boundary lines have fallen for me in pleasant places;*
> *surely I have a delightful inheritance.*

> *I will praise the Lord, who counsels me;*
> *even at night my heart instructs me.*

> *I keep my eyes always on the Lord.*
> *With him at my right hand, I will not be shaken.*

Don't let a broken heart sabotage your ability to believe what a loving God has put in print for you. Trust Him to mend it. In fact, trust him with your life and death.

Love originates from God and motivates us to do whatever it takes to identify the key that enables our children to connect with others. Whether it is music, seashells, or drawing, pursuing a special interest can unearth that key and enable them to have vital relationships, emotional and spiritual well-being, purpose, and vocation. Seek to carefully define success personally, in your parenting, and for your children until they can do so for themselves. One family defined success for their medically fragile son as hours interceding in prayer for those he watched on the news from his bed. For your child, success might be finding a school where he is appreciated, getting up out of bed in time for a healthy breakfast, or clearing the beach of litter. Articulating what success looks like will help you recognize it when it arrives.

*What does success look like for you this week?*

*What does success look like for your child today?*

*What will successful parenting look like for you when your children are adults?*

# 15

*"Get Over Your Cheap Self"*

It's Not About You

*by Jim Moriarty*

## "Get Over Your Cheap Self"

*Allie spent two weeks in Italy at a music camp. High school students from around the world experienced the ubiquitous music on every cobblestone street in Europe, international travel, master classes, and mounds of gelato. As Allie got off the plane, she told us, "I drink coffee now."*

*Musically, the take-home message from the whole adventure was to, "get over your cheap self." The instructors used this cheeky expression to help the musicians overcome the self-consciousness that can sabotage a performance. In order to get on stage and perform well, one has to stop worrying about how your hair looks, whether you picked the right black dress, and even how you sound. A truly accomplished performer is focused on the piece of music and the experience they want to create for the audience.*

*When we have gotten over our cheap selves, we have more to give our children. Pride can be subtle or crass, manifesting in the form of nervous laughter or debilitating embarrassment. Our kids' most challenging behaviors can be the antidote that cleanses us of impure motives and cures us of inadvertently making demands on them to make us look good. Serving our kids as sacrificially as is sometimes necessary, requires the removal of every shred of pride. I'm letting Jim write this chapter because, well, I'm still working on this one.*

# 15

## It's Not About You

*As a busker, one thing that does not work is self-conscious-ness. A busker needs to shed all ego and get down to work. Play your songs, play them well, earn your money, and don't get in people's way.*

—GLEN HANSARD, IRISH SINGER-SONGWRITER

M usic makes Reid's world go around, but it's not the only thing he does. He thoroughly enjoys playing baseball on the Storm team every Saturday. Admittedly, the local radio announcer, Ernie, makes it for him with his professional play-by-play commentary. Reid sits cross-legged leaning on the backstop to be close to Ernie. Sometimes he turns his back on the game to face the media console and watch Ernie depress the push-to-talk microphone, adjust the scoreboard to a permanent tie game, and select music for the inning stretches.

I'll never forget the first time I walked up our hill to one of his first Miracle League[22] baseball games. I arrived as one person and left someone else.

I grew up playing baseball; my dad coached my team as well as the teams of my two brothers before me. I played first base, was on an all-star team or two, the whole nine yards. I thought I knew Little League baseball inside and out. These were my peeps more than some of the groups of special needs families Andrea had dragged me to in the past. However, what I saw as I walked up that hill was not at all familiar. The scene I encountered was a rather motley crew of dozens of kids with myriad disabilities, playing a game that only somewhat resembled the game I knew.

It was like seeing a sport played in a foreign country. Baseball has three outfielders and one person playing second base, I thought. It is defined by four balls, three strikes, and a final score. We've come to understand that it's a highly competitive game that brings out the best in kids and the worst in parents. Youth sports are in large part an extension of us as parents; we want to win so we push our kids, sometimes very hard, to win on our behalf. We are raised to believe Red Sanders who said, "Winning isn't everything, it's the only thing."

At Miracle League everything was different. The field was crowded. As many as six people clustered around each base; others roamed aimlessly in the outfield. Various wheelchair styles were represented, and parents came in and out of the dugouts to tie shoes or tuck in shirts. Every player had a buddy. Every player got a hit, and even those who couldn't hold a bat somehow managed to get on base with the help of their buddy. Every player

---

22 The Miracle League believes that every child deserves a chance to play baseball and has a mission to provide that opportunity through 275 organizations across the world. themiracleleague.net

scored a run and every two-inning game was a tie. For all these reasons, it took a few minutes for it to happen that day but not more than ten.

Very quickly, I shed my preconceived notions and realized one simple fact: it wasn't about me. That may sound small or insignificant, but it was huge. Everything flipped 180 degrees in my mind. I went that day believing baseball was about one team winning and another losing. I thought the game was about statistics, strikeouts, big hits, and high-drama clutch plays. In those few minutes, I realized that America's definition of baseball is bunk. I know that sounds like heresy. The silly game of baseball wasn't about what I had been told. Baseball is about playing with friends, caring about your teammates, and having fun. The kids in Miracle League don't know how to taunt the other team and jeer them to fail. They cheer on the opposing team.

The scene that day demanded that I look beyond myself, discount my own feelings, and put aside my need to look good to anyone, or everyone else. It required an internal transformation for me to see the kids for who they are. Once I was able to do that, I saw such beautiful things that I go back for another fix every week… every year…for years…even when Reid can't make a game due to a scheduling conflict.

After those few minutes, I saw the kids' joy.

I saw their stoke for the game they were playing.

I saw their camaraderie.

I saw their hearts not their outward appearance.

I saw selfless giving.

I saw love like I'd never associated with the game of baseball. These kids were not there to pay off the Red Sanders quote. It's likely none of them had ever truly "won" anything because they weren't involved in win-lose activities.

It can bring you to tears if you think about it very long. Andrea summed it up in spiritual terms. What makes Miracle League miraculous is that everyone is both a winner and a loser, depending on your prerogative. It is a picture of heaven, where we will "all have sinned and fall short of the glory of God" (Romans 3:23). Yet, through Christ's free gift of salvation, we are all welcomed in to play for eternity. We've all lost, yet we all win, just like Miracle League.

⟶᧚

The profound lesson I learned was that life wasn't about me. Honestly, I couldn't see that for a while because I was too busy thinking about myself; that realization sums up my journey of being Reid's dad. Associating closely with a disabled child often flies in the face of what our culture prizes: intelligence, excellence, achievement, and accomplishment. Only once we get over ourselves, can we stand in righteous defiance that they are also qualified for life on this planet. Andrea will tell you she watched me change from being angry and annoyed to become loving and accepting, and willing to come alongside Reid and others to see life from their perspective. At the fulcrum of that pivot was an utter helplessness that I had to confront.

I had entered parenthood self-centered, arrogant, and focused on myself, just as I approached the baseball diamond that day. America celebrates that mindset. I had been successful in business. I was traveling, frequently internationally, and I had married the love of my life. All was well. Everyone around me saw me as successful. I was living the American dream, complete with home ownership at a young age. I was ready for the next chapter: to take on the role of being a dad. I wasn't going to be a typical dad. I was planning to be an amazing dad. I thought I knew what that meant because I had grown up with an awesome dad. Having watched him, I figured all I had to do was mirror what he had done. This started to become reality with the birth of our twins, yet looking back I missed a few major points. I wanted to be an awesome dad more than I actually wanted to meet my kids' wants, needs, and desires. If we're honest with ourselves, I think we all have these qualities. I may just have had them in larger helpings.

When I became a dad, I was ready to skateboard with my kids, teach them to surf, introduce them to all kinds of music, and take them on trips overseas. Mostly, I was ready to mold my kids into my own image. That's how I walked up to that baseball game: ready to be the same awesome coach my dad had been. But I had missed a key attribute. My dad was there for me, not for himself. I had yet to learn this lesson. I was ready to see the game through my own eyes. What crystalized in my mind that day was how flawed that approach is. Forcing things into your own worldview does not yield the greatest result. It is only when we see how shallow and self-centered our own mindset is that we can see beyond it. I might have just picked up Rick Warren's *The Purpose Driven Life*; he summarized all of the above in his opening sentence, "It's not about you."

That baseball game sticks in my mind because it offers a succinct, encapsulated summary of my years as a dad. My inwardly focused approach was wrong. The times I've come closest to fully realizing who God wants me to be as a dad are when I put others' wants, needs, and desires before my own. Instead of forcing my kids to take up skateboarding and surfing, two things that I love dearly, I learned that my life became richer when I explored what my kids were into. Allie fell in love with ice skating at an early age. I thought it was a bit odd since we lived in San Diego, but I guess no more so than my becoming a surfer in northeastern Ohio. Many Saturdays at the rink, and later riding horses, I would wait, watching her and attentively taking photos. Those were moments when my life started to pivot away from selfish pursuit toward selfless love.

As I leaned into this new mindset, I could embrace Allie's true gift of playing music. She was practicing flute and piccolo daily and playing in the San Diego Youth Symphony as a teen. In high school, she taught music to underprivileged kids near the Mexican border. Her life vector was forming in front of our eyes.

The story with Reid, as you now know, is much the same. I cannot sing (in tune anyway). Andrea was discouraged from buying albums as a teenager because of subversive lyrics. Neither of us have fronted a band or recorded a song, let alone an album. When we, as a team, started to get out of the way and enable Reid's gifts to blossom with people who were strong influences in his life his mission started to form. I could have tried harder to force him to surf, but why? The cost might have been in the areas he's flourishing.

One doesn't become a dad the day your kids are born. I believe we become dads (and moms) when we truly embrace our kids for who they are rather than who we thought we wanted them to be. In truth, if you force your kids to become mini-mes, you're bound to be let down because your view of yourself is probably not based in reality. It will be impossible for your child to achieve. More importantly, their heart and their true God-given gifts are slightly different than yours. They are not you, and we should truly thank God for that. Life is richer because of our differences, not our similarities.

*What expectations do you have of your child?*

*How is your child different from you?*

*What life lessons have you learned from your child?*

*\*One Final Note...*

Have you answered all the questions at the end of the chapters? I encourage you to review them now and treat them as a journal of sorts. As you compile them, be discerning. They may reveal clues, patterns, and directions for you. You could save them in a computer document or write them on Post-it notes to stick around your kitchen. Taken as a whole collection, they may lead you to affirm your child's strengths, pray for mentors, have a working dinner with your spouse, write a story, or spend time alone with God. Use them to intentionally unlock and amplify your child's passion as you help them find their purpose at every stage in life.

# The Magic of Music Therapy

There are seven reasons I think music therapy is the magic in our story. Reid's affinity was for music, which has its own therapy. If your child's affinity is for trains, the challenge for you is to design a train therapy—not necessarily board-certified—to do these things for them. I believe it can be done and would love to hear what you come up with or brainstorm with you online.

Music therapy:

1. Addresses practically any IEP goal.
2. Is innately pleasurable; music is its own reward.
3. Employs a relative strength.
4. Utilizes the whole brain.
5. Adapts through one's lifespan.
6. Generalizes easily outside the clinic.
7. Allows for structure and creativity simultaneously.

# Life in Review Song Lists

*Music is the soundtrack of your life.*

—DICK CLARK

Allie had an intriguing assignment at Berklee College of Music upon declaring her major in music therapy: make a list of ten songs that define who you are. I couldn't resist including one for each member of our family with an invitation for you to make your own.

## ALLIE'S LIFE IN REVIEW

1. "I Wish" by Stevie Wonder
2. "You Can Call Me Al" by Paul Simon
3. "Deep in the Hundred Acre Wood" by Richard and Robert Sherman
4. "Sonata" by Poulenc
5. "Carmen Suite" by Bizet
6. "It Is Well with my Soul" by Horatio Spafford
7. "Chim Chim Cheree" by Richard and Robert Sherman

8. "Shine" by Reid Moriarty
9. "When I'm With You" by Best Coast
10. "Moondance" by Van Morrison

## REID'S LIFE IN REVIEW

1. "Apple Apple" by Barbara Milne
2. "No Gluten" by Michelle Lazar
3. "My First Hymnal" by Karyn Henley
4. "Ways to Say Hello" by Angela Neve
5. "Love's in Need of Love Today" by Stevie Wonder
6. "Shine" by Reid Moriarty
7. "Shackles (Praise You)" by Mary Mary
8. "Chim Chim Cheree" by Richard and Robert Sherman
9. "Hallelujahs" by Chris Rice
10. "Here in the Real World" by George Jones

## JIM'S LIFE IN REVIEW

1. "Changes" by David Bowie
2. "Washington Bullets" by The Clash
3. "Fairytale of New York" by The Pogues
4. "Righteous Rocking" by Lee Scratch Perry
5. "God Only Knows" by The Beach Boys
6. "It's Oh So Quiet" by Bjork
7. "Better" by Regina Spektor

8. "Low Rising" by The Swell Season
9. "Morning" by Beck
10. "Magnetized" by Wilco

## ANDREA'S LIFE IN REVIEW

1. "Sweet Baby James" by James Taylor
2. "Everyday" by Buddy Holly
3. "Everyday I Write the Book" by Elvis Costello
4. "Hymns to the Silence" by Van Morrison
5. "Tell Me Why" lullaby by author unknown
6. "Sir Duke" by Stevie Wonder
7. "Standing in the Gap" by Babbie Mason
8. "Revelation Song" by Kari Jobe
9. "I Have a Maker (He Knows My Name)" by Paul Baloche
10. "My Lighthouse" by Rend Collective

# Resources

Armstrong, Thomas. *Neurodiversity: Discovering the Extraordinary Gifts of Autism, ADHD, Dyslexia, and Other Brain Differences.* Cambridge, MA: Da Capo Lifelong, 2010.

Barnett, Kristine. *The Spark: A Mother's Story of Nurturing Genius.* New York: Random House, 2014.

Bianco, Margery Williams, and Michael Hague. *The Velveteen Rabbit, Or, How Toys Become Real.* New York: Holt, Rinehart and Winston, 1983.

Chapman, Gary D., and Ross Campbell. *The Five Love Languages of Children.* Chicago: Moody, 1997.

Colbert, Stephen. (2015, September). The Purpose of Joy and Laughter [video file]. Retrieved from https://www.youtube.com/watch?v=w3XE6EK7MV8

Dennis, Randall, and Karyn Henley. *My First Hymnal.* Nashville, TN: Sparrow, 1994.

Dickson, Sue, Jeanette Cason, and Marjorie Knapp. *Sing, Spell, Read & Write: A Total Language Arts Curriculum*. Parsippany, NJ: Modern Curriculum, 1998.

Florance, Cheri L. and Marin Gazzaniga. *Maverick Mind: A Mother's Story of Solving the Mystery of her Unreachable, Unteachable, Silent Son*. New York: G.P. Putnam's Sons, 2004.

Foreman, Mark, and Jan Foreman. *Never Say No: Raising Big-picture Kids*. Colorado Springs, CO: David C. Cook, 2015.

Gill, Barbara. *Changed by a Child: Companion Notes for Parents of a Child with a Disability*. New York: Doubleday, 1997.

Green, Steve. Hide 'em in Your Heart series. Sparrow, 1990.

Guy, Julie and Angela Neve. *In Harmony*. www.inharmonylearning. com.

Howland, K. (2015, May). How Music Can Heal Our Brain and Heart [video file]. Retrieved from https://www.youtube.com/ watch?v=NlY4yCsGKXU

Jiang, Jia. *Rejection Proof: How I Beat Fear and Became Invincible, One Rejection at a Time*. New York: Random House USA, 2015.

Joel's Vision Arts. www.joelsvisionarts.com.

Kluth, Paula, and Patrick Schwarz. *Just Give Him the Whale!: 20 Ways to Use Fascinations, Areas of Expertise, and Strengths to Support Students with Autism*. Baltimore: Paul H. Brookes Pub., 2008.

Kohn, Alfie. *Punished by Rewards: The Trouble with Gold Stars, Incentive Plans, A's, Praise, and Other Bribes.* Boston: Houghton Mifflin, 1993.

Kraus, Robert and Jose Aruego. *Leo the Late Bloomer.* London: Windmill Books, 1971.

Lazar, Michelle. *Tuned Into Learning.* www.tunedintolearning.com.

Lears, Laurie, and Karen Ritz. *Ian's Walk: A Story about Autism.* Morton Grove, IL: Albert Whitman, 1998.

Milne, Barbara. *Sounds Like Fun. 2010.* www.barbaramilne.com.

Model Me Kids. www.modelmekids.com.

Moore, Beth. *The Inheritance: Here and Now.* Nashville: Lifeway. 2010.

Moore, Beth. *Living Free: Learning to Pray God's Word.* Nashville: Lifeway. 2001.

Papatola, D. (2009, September 4). Guys who wrote tunes for 'Poppins' film
also penned a love-it-or-hate-it pop tune. *Twin Cities Pioneer Press.* Retrieved from http://www.twincities.com/ci_13261119

Peterson, Eugene H. *The Message: The Bible in Contemporary Language.* NavPress: Colorado Springs, 2004.

Rogers, Judy. *Go to the Ant,* P & R Publishing, 1989.

Rath, Tom, and Marcus Buckingham. *StrengthsFinder 2.0*. New York: Gallup, 2007.

Sandford, John. *Slappy Hooper: The World's Greatest Sign Painter*. Grand Haven, MI: Dogs in Hats Children's, 2004.

Simon, Rachel. *Riding the Bus with My Sister*. New York: Grand Central Publishing, 2013.

Suskind, Ron. *Life, Animated: A Story of Sidekicks, Heroes, and Autism*. Glendale, CA: Kingswell, 2014.

The Songstream Project: Music as a Vehicle. "Voices of Autism." http://thesongstreamproject.org/index.php/shows/voices-of-autism

Talk Time with Reid Moriarty. www.reidmoriarty.com.

Vagin, Anna. *Movie Time Social Learning: Using Movies to Teach Social Thinking and Social Understanding*. San Jose, CA: Social Thinking, 2012.

Vagin, Anna. *YouCue Feelings: Using Online Videos for Social Learning*. Charleston, SC: CreateSpace, 2015.

Varga, G. (2015, July 4). Switchfoot opening music school for kids. *San Diego Union Tribune*. Retrieved from http://www.sandiegouniontribune.com

Warner, Gertrude Chandler. *The Boxcar Children*. Chicago: Albert Whitman, 1977.

Warren, Richard. *The Purpose-driven Life: What on Earth Am I Here For?* Grand Rapids, MI: Zondervan, 2002.

"Westminster Shorter Catechism." *Westminster Shorter Catechism.* Center for Reformed Theology and Apologetics, 1647.

Zander, Rosamund Stone, and Benjamin Zander. *The Art of Possibility.* Boston, MA: Harvard Business School, 2000.

# Acknowledgments

I am so grateful for every single babysitter, therapist, tutor, doctor, neighbor, bus driver, respite worker, counselor, coach, and friend who makes up the metropolis it has taken to get Reid where he is today. They are literally too numerous to mention.

A smaller group of cherished friends helped me finish this book:

I would like to thank Vanessa and Talia for perceiving Reid's life as a compelling story and sharing their stage with me.

What more can I say about Angela? Obviously, we love her. Thank you for serving, leading, and singing with all of us.

Many thanks to my insightful writing coach, Marni. She was the angel sent to say, "You need to put God in the book."

I appreciate Sandi for paving the way and always having time to brainstorm.

To the Facebook friends who were my first excited editors, thank you.

To Tracy Jones for being a thorough and trustworthy editor, thank you.

Haleigh, though we didn't speak, I appreciated your meticulous insight and sincerely hope you can edit my next book.

To Carla, a million thanks for the million phone calls. I have never even heard of a better listener than this woman whom I chose first as Reid's tutor, then as my friend, and now a sister.

Thank you to my mom for investing in our family and modeling how to make a way when there isn't one.

I am so very grateful for Allie. She both "gets me" and has "got me."

To Reid, thank you for being you.

Jim is my greatest champion. I thank him for being my collaborator, muse, and so much more. Everyday.

Lastly, I offer eternal thanks to the unseen God who is always present, always on the move, and always speaking to us. I am so grateful for His Word.

# About the Author

Andrea Moriarty is the cofounder of the music therapy nonprofit Banding Together and blogs at AutismUnplugged.com. Her refreshing, spiritual take on both the challenges and triumphs of parenting a differently abled child offers affectionate humor and unending hope.

Moriarty and her husband Jim are the proud adoptive parents of twins Allie and Reid. Allie currently studies music education and music therapy at Berklee College of Music in Boston. Reid makes music, performs regularly, and hosts his own podcast: *Talk Time with Reid Moriarty*.

Moriarty lives in Solana Beach, California, where she accumulates books, cooks from scratch, and whistles while she works.

# What's your favorite color?

Reid and Angela have a collection of songs about every color in the rainbow. What's even better, the proceeds benefit the music therapy nonprofit Banding Together.

*"I like the green song because it takes care of the earth."*
Julian, age 7

*"The purple song is awesome, I love it!"*
Declan, age 4

*"My son was struggling to learn colors, pairing these songs with objects helped him learn them."*
Jodie, teacher and mom

**Available at reidmoriarty.com and iTunes.**

# TALK TIME *with* Reid Moriarty

*Talk Time with Reid Moriarty* is a series of biweekly podcasts with people Reid finds interesting, and you might too! Each one is 7-9 minutes long and will inform and delight you at the same time.

Guests include Ralph Rubio, Murray Monster, Keb' Mo', Babbie Mason, and Mark Foreman.

**Tune in at ReidMoriarty.com or on Soundcloud**

Made in the USA
Charleston, SC
09 August 2016